FOCUS ON THE FAMILY PRESENTS

Adventures in
ODYSSEY®

90 DeVoTiONS for KiDS

MARSHAL YOUNGER, CREATIVE DIRECTOR

Tyndale House Publishers, Inc.
Carol Stream, Illinois

90 Devotions for Kids

Copyright © 2012 Focus on the Family

A Focus on the Family book published by
Tyndale House Publishers, Inc., Carol Stream, Illinois 60188

Focus on the Family and Adventures in Odyssey, and the accompanying logos and designs, are
federally registered trademarks of Focus on the Family, Colorado Springs, CO 80995.

TYNDALE and Tyndale's quill logo are registered trademarks of Tyndale House Publishers, Inc.

Unless otherwise noted, Scripture quotations are taken from the *Holy Bible, New International
Reader's Version*®, NIrV® Copyright © 1995, 1996, 1998 by Biblica, Inc.™ Used by permission of
Zondervan. www.zondervan.com. All Scripture quotations marked NIV are taken from the *Holy
Bible, New International Version*®. NIV®. Copyright © 1973, 1978, 1984 by Biblica, Inc.™ Used by
permission of Zondervan. All rights reserved worldwide. www.zondervan.com.

The poem on page 120 is used by permission of Simple Literature. Copyright © 2012 by Simple
Literature.

No part of this publication may be reproduced, stored in a retrieval system, or transmitted in any
form or by any means—electronic, mechanical, photocopy, recording, or otherwise—without prior
written permission of Focus on the Family.

Editor: Marianne Hering
Cover design by Jacqueline L. Nuñez
Cover illustration and interior illustrations of characters by Gary Locke
Interior design by Lexie Rhodes

ISBN: 978-1-58997-682-5

Printed in the United States of America

6 7 8 9 /18

For manufacturing information regarding this product, please call 1-800-323-9400.

Contents

How to Use These Devotions, by John Avery Whittaker.....................1

Theme 1—Salvation (Ephesians 2:5)
by Marshal Younger

1 What Salvation Is Not (*Ephesians 2:8*) 4

2 What Salvation Is (*2 Corinthians 5:17*)............................6

3 The Perfect Place (*John 14:2*)......................................8

4 And That's Not All! (*John 10:10*).................................10

5 "What Must I Do to Be Saved?" (*Romans 10:9–10*).................12

6 Baptism (*Matthew 3:16*)..14

7 "Okay, I'm Dry. What Now?" (*Luke 2:52*).........................16

Theme 2—Learning About Jesus (John 8:12)
by Kathy Buchanan

8 A Not-So-Royal Welcome (*Mark 10:45*)............................22

9 A Holy Lot of Fish and Bread (*Matthew 19:26*)....................24

10 Going Out on a Limb (*Luke 19:10*)...............................26

11 Being Sheepish (*John 10:11*)......................................28

12 The Rest of the Time (*Psalm 46:10*) 30

13 Doing the Unexpected (*John 11:25*)..............................32

14 Hope Returned (*John 3:16*) 34

Theme 3—Discipleship (Ephesians 5:1)
by Jeanne Gowen Dennis

15 Just Like Whit (*2 Corinthians 3:18*).............................40

16 Try, Try Again (*2 Timothy 1:7*)..................................42

17 Stand Strong (*1 Corinthians 16:13–14*)...........................44

18 Everything for Jesus (*Matthew 16:24*) 46

19 Different for Jesus (*1 Peter 1:14–15*) 48

20 Even the Greatest Obeyed (*2 Corinthians 10:5*) 50

21 Jesus, Not Me (*1 Peter 5:6*) 52

Theme 4—Prayer (1 Thessalonians 5:17)
by Marshal Younger

22 The Best Friend (*Psalm 5:3*) 58

23 How to Pray, Part I: Thanksgiving and Praise (*Psalm 100:4*) 60

24 How to Pray, Part II: Confession (*1 John 1:9*) 62

25 How to Pray, Part III: Intercession (*James 5:16*) 64

26 How to Pray, Part IV: Petition (*Philippians 4:6*) 66

27 "I'm Starving!" (*Ezra 8:21*) 68

28 Unanswered Prayers (*Romans 11:33*) 70

Theme 5—The Bible (Psalm 119:89)
by Marshal Younger

29 What's the Big Deal About the Bible? (*Isaiah 40:8*) 76

30 What's in the Bible? (*Hebrews 4:12*) 78

31 So How Should You Read the Bible? (*Proverbs 2:2*) 80

32 Studying the Bible (*2 Timothy 3:16*) 82

33 What Does the Bible Mean? (*Psalm 119:73*) 84

34 Bible Memorization (*Psalm 119:11*) 86

35 "So What's It to Me?" (*Ephesians 6:17*) 88

Theme 6—Exercising Faith (Hebrews 11:1)
by Marshal Younger

36 What Is Faith? (*2 Chronicles 20:20*) 94

37 The Power of Faith (*Mark 5:34*) 96

38 "Dude, Where's My Faith?" (*1 Thessalonians 5:16–18*) 98

39 Faith and Science (*Psalm 139:14*) 100

40 Faith Through the Tough Stuff (*Psalm 30:5*) 102

41 The Silent Singer (*James 2:14*) 104

42 That Last Step Is a Doozy! (*Proverbs 16:3*) 106

Theme 7—Forgiveness (Ephesians 4:32)
by Sheila Seifert

43 The Public Defender (*Psalm 103:10*) 112

44 Live Fully (*Luke 6:37*) 114

45 Socks and Showers (*Luke 17:3*) 116

46 A Historical Apology (*Matthew 6:12*) 118

47 Asking for Forgiveness (*Romans 12:18*) 120

48 The Full Apology (*Acts 2:38*) 122

49 Running from Yourself (*1 John 2:12*) 124

Theme 8—Giving (Acts 20:35)
by Marshal Younger

50 In Rod We Trust? (*Proverbs 3:9*) 130

51 Mine! (*Hebrews 13:16*) 132

52 Generosity (*2 Corinthians 9:7*) 134

53 God, the Provider (*Philippians 4:19*) 136

54 Greed (*1 Timothy 6:10*) 138

55 Other Stuff to Give (*1 Peter 4:10*) 140

56 Giving When It Hurts (*Psalm 4:5*) 142

Theme 9—Witnessing (Matthew 28:19–20)
by Marshal Younger

57 The Words of Life (*Romans 1:1*) 148

58 Earning Your Right to Speak (*1 Peter 2:12*) 150

59 How to Witness (*Mark 1:17*) 152

60 Your Personal Testimony (*1 Peter 3:15*) 154
61 That Guy (*Matthew 5:16*) 156
62 Missionaries to Main Street (*Acts 1:8*) 158
63 Looking for Opportunities (*Colossians 4:5*) 160

Theme 10—Worship (Psalm 99:5)
by Marshal Younger

64 Ways to Worship (*Psalm 109:30*) 166
65 Nuts About P-Nut (*Psalm 30:12*) 168
66 The Names of God (*Luke 1:49*) 170
67 Worthy of Worship, Part I: God's Power (*Psalm 18:2*) 170
68 Worthy of Worship, Part II: God's Wisdom (*Job 12:13*) 174
69 Whacked-Out Worship (*1 Corinthians 10:14*) 176
70 Worthy of Worship, Part III: God's Love (*1 John 4:9*) 178

Theme 11—Going to Church (1 Corinthians 12:27)
by Sheila Seifert

71 More Than a Building? (*Matthew 16:18*) 184
72 A Part of the Whole (*Ephesians 4:16*) 186
73 Listen and Learn (*Proverbs 1:5*) 188
74 Rules and Consequences (*Proverbs 3:1–2*) 190
75 No Side Effects (*Hebrews 10:25*) 192
76 Sticks and Strength (*Ecclesiastes 4:12*) 194
77 The Power of God's Presence (*Acts 2:42*) 196

Theme 12—Serving Others (Matthew 25:40)
by Bob Smithouser

78 Love for the Least (*1 Corinthians 13:3*) 202
79 Me Third = Joy (*1 Corinthians 10:24*) 204
80 Only the Lonely (*Isaiah 53:3*) 206

81 Set Your World on Fire (*Ephesians 6:7*). 208

82 Ten Thirsty Camels (*Galatians 6:10*). 210

83 Someone Else's Cleats (*Zechariah 7:9*) 212

84 Follow the Leader (*Matthew 20:28*). 214

Theme 13—Overcoming Sin (Romans 3:23–24)
by Marshal Younger

85 It's All Around Us (*Romans 6:12*) 220

86 The Consequences (*James 1:14–15*) 222

87 The Most Important Person (*Galatians 5:13–14*) 224

88 "Getting Away" with Sin (*Proverbs 28:13*). 226

89 Don't Fly Toward the Light! (*Philippians 4:8*) 228

90 Really Sorry (*Luke 5:32*) 230

Special Bonus Devo!

"We, the Jury, Find the Defendant . . . Guilty!" (*Romans 5:18*). 232

A Final Word from Whit 236

How to Use These Devotions

by John Avery Whittaker

I've found that one of the best ways to study the Bible is with friends. Especially my friends in Odyssey. Connie, Eugene, Wooton . . . we'd regularly meet at Whit's End to read and talk. The three of them bring unique perspectives that add a lot to my understanding of Scripture and enrich my faith. So I had the idea of putting together a devotional book that brings the Bible and my friends together. Friends like you.

There are thirteen themes in this devotional—biblical themes we thought were important as we studied our Bibles. Each theme has an introduction, seven devotions, a memory verse, a challenge for you personally (or to use with your family), and an even more challenging puzzle to help you remember what you've learned.

You can work on the theme's memory verse for all seven devotions—or you can memorize it the very first day of the theme. You can do the puzzle anytime you want, though some of the puzzles won't make sense if you do them before you read all the devotions in that week's theme.

You'll need your Bible for many of the challenges, so you may want to keep it nearby.

Do you have to read a devotion every day? No. This book is here whenever you want to use it. But remember: Spending time in the Bible is a good habit to have. You should try to do it every day. It keeps you connected to God—and helps you grow in your faith.

One last thing: When we use the word *story* in reference to the Bible, we mean a true historical account from the pages of Scripture. The Bible is not a book of myths, tall tales, or legends. It's true, every word of it.

Well, Eugene, Connie, and Wooton are waiting. Let's get started, shall we?

Salvation

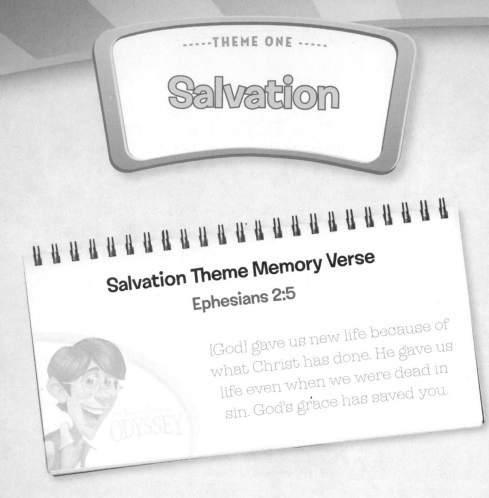

Salvation Theme Memory Verse
Ephesians 2:5

[God] gave us new life because of what Christ has done. He gave us life even when we were dead in sin. God's grace has saved you.

It was as if a bomb went off. The walls and ceiling shook. The prison doors broke open. The chains on Paul's and Silas's feet came loose.

It was an earthquake, and the jailer woke to see all the doors wide open. It was his job to keep the doors locked and the prisoners inside. He thought all of the prisoners were gone. He knew that he would be punished if they escaped.

Rather than wait for the punishment, he drew his sword to kill himself. But Paul shouted, "Don't do it! We're all still here. Just don't kill yourself!"

The jailer was moved by their concern for him. The God of Paul and Silas—the One who had caused the earthquake—was also a God of compassion. God's loving-kindness was the reason Paul and Silas were being compassionate. The jailer wanted this compassionate God for himself. So he asked Paul, "What must I do to be saved?" (See Acts 16:24–34 for the whole story.)

• • •

Being "saved" is the most important decision a person will ever make. Phrases like "let Jesus come into your heart," "accept Jesus as your Savior," and "be born again" are all talking about the same thing—salvation.

But what does salvation mean? Why should you accept salvation? And if you decide you want to be saved, how do you go about it? Those topics will be explored all this week. And if you want the God in your life who can create an earthquake and offer undeserved compassion—all in the same night—just ask yourself the question, "What must I do to be saved?"

Prayer

Dear God,

Thank You for the salvation that You offer all of us. Thank You for offering me compassion that I don't deserve. Help me to fully understand this gift.

Amen.

Devo 1

What Salvation Is Not

Today's Verse—Ephesians 2:8

God's grace has saved you because of your faith in Christ. Your salvation doesn't come from anything you do. It is God's gift.

Two boys wanted a drink of water. The first boy mowed someone's lawn so that he could earn enough money to buy a shovel. With the shovel, he dug a well in his backyard. Exhausted, he finally hit water, and the well filled up. Then he mowed three more lawns so that he could earn enough money for the rigging that would lower a bucket into the well and pull up water.

Next, he cut down a tree in his backyard, peeled the bark off the thin branches, and braided them together to create his own rope. With the rope, he could lower the bucket into the well and retrieve the water. He also took glass-blowing classes so that he could learn how to make his own drinking glass.

After two weeks of backbreaking work, the boy finally got his glass of water. He lowered the bucket into the ten-foot well he had dug and drew the water out of the well with the rope he had fashioned. He poured the water into the glass he had made, and then he took a very long drink.

The second boy went to a water fountain, turned it on, and drank all the water he wanted.

The first boy worked hard for his glass of water, but salvation cannot be earned by hard work. We cannot earn salvation by going to church, or reading the Bible a lot, or praying a lot, or being nice to people. All of those things are good, but salvation isn't something we can work for.

Salvation is like the water fountain. It's a gift. Jesus has already done the work for

Connie's Corner

Yesterday, for some reason, Whit's End had no customers for hours! So I swept the floor, washed down all the machines twice, and rearranged the menu board so that the ice-cream flavors were in order of popularity. Poor black cherry!

I guess I kept myself busy because I felt guilty for getting paid for doing nothing. It also took me awhile to accept that I did nothing to deserve my salvation either. But I shouldn't feel guilty. Salvation is free.

us on the cross. Just as the second boy gladly accepted the water from the fountain, all we need to do is accept God's gift of salvation by putting our faith in Jesus.

Daily Challenge

Read John 19, the story about Jesus' trial and crucifixion on the cross. That was the "work" Jesus did for you. Thank God in prayer for His sacrifice.

• • •

Salvation Theme Memory Verse—Ephesians 2:5

[God] gave us new life because of what Christ has done. He gave us life even when we were dead in sin. God's grace has saved you.

Devo 2

What Salvation Is

Today's Verse—2 Corinthians 5:17

Anyone who believes in Christ is a new creation.
The old is gone! The new has come!

In the *Adventures in Odyssey* episode* "Imagination Station Revisited, I and II" (album 50), Kelly didn't understand why Jesus had to die on a cross. For the answer to that question, let's go back to the beginning. And by "back," I mean W-A-A-A-Y back.

God created Adam and Eve. When they were created, the world was perfect: no pain, no death, no math homework. How great is that? But then Satan showed up and tempted Adam and Eve to disobey God. When Adam and Eve took bites of the fruit that God told them not to eat, they brought sin into the world. The world was no longer perfect. Romans 6:23 says, "When you sin, the pay you get is death." This means that, because of sin, all humans have to die. All of us sin (Romans 3:23), so every person dies.

But this is the cool part. Romans 6:23 doesn't end with death. The verse ends with "but God gives you the gift of eternal life because of what Christ Jesus our Lord has done." God sent His Son Jesus to earth for a lot of reasons. Jesus came to teach, to heal, and to show His love for everyone. But the main reason He came to earth was to die in our place. Jesus took all of our sin on Himself and died on the cross so that we don't have to pay the consequences for our sins. We can have eternal life in heaven because of God's gift of His Son's life.

Salvation is when we first believe in our hearts that Jesus did this for us. We ask for His forgiveness and His gift of eternal life. When we do that, we are given the gift of Jesus in our life—and what a life that is! Not only is it the best life we can imagine; it's

---

* For more information about air dates for Adventures in Odyssey® audio dramas, visit *www.whits end.org* and click on "Radio."

Loquacious Learning with Eugene

The word *salvation* comes from a Greek word that means "to deliver." "Deliver" in this sense isn't like delivering mail. It's what God did when He brought Moses and the Israelites out of slavery in Egypt. The word *deliver* could be translated "to rescue." We are, in essence, "rescued" from sin when we're saved. We are definitely not "mailed" from sin. That would be utterly preposterous.

an eternal life. And then we offer up our lives to Him. We tell God that we are going to try to live the way He wants us to live.

When we are saved, we're called a "new creation." Luke 19 talks about a man named Zacchaeus. You remember, he's the "wee little man" from the old Sunday school song. Zacchaeus was a tax collector who cheated people out of their money. He had no friends. But then one day, he climbed a tree to see Jesus, and Jesus noticed him. Jesus showed that He loved Zacchaeus even though no one else did. Jesus came over for dinner, and Zacchaeus decided to do the right thing. He gave back all the money he had stolen, and more. His life was changed because of Jesus. In verse 9, Jesus said to Zacchaeus, "Today salvation has come to your house." When salvation comes to us, our lives are changed too.

Daily Challenge

Find and read the Bible stories about these people: Zacchaeus (Luke 19), Paul (Acts 22), and Nicodemus (John 3). All three of these men were delivered from something. What were they delivered from?

• • •

Salvation Theme Memory Verse—Ephesians 2:5

[God] gave us new life because of what Christ has done. He gave us life even when we were dead in sin. God's grace has saved you.

The Perfect Place

Today's Verse—John 14:2

There are many rooms in my Father's house.
If this were not true, I would have told you. I am
going there to prepare a place for you.

Recently, *Odyssey* fan Payton H. described what would be the perfect day for her. She mentioned a trip to New Zealand, roller coasters, and "my favorite movie star feeding me watermelon." What would be a perfect day for you? Unlimited ice cream? A day at the beach? Sitting behind home plate watching your favorite team win the seventh game of the World Series?

As good as all of those things are, being in heaven will be so much better than any of that. In fact, we can't even imagine the joy we'll experience in heaven. First Corinthians 2:9 says, "No eye has seen, no ear has heard, no mind has known what God has prepared for those who love him."

We don't know exactly what it will be like in heaven, but we're given a few clues in the Bible. Revelation 5 talks about hearing the voices of singing angels. Revelation 21 tells us that there will be no more crying or death or pain. But the best thing about heaven will be the presence of God. In fact, Revelation 22 tells us that there won't even be a need for the sun in heaven, because God will be bright enough to light up the whole place.

People often wonder if heaven is going to be boring. When it comes down to it, heaven does sound a lot like never-ending church. Church is nice, but all day, every day? And for eternity? Wow. That's a lot of singing. But the problem is probably our lack of imagination.

Ginny was a woman who had been blind since birth. She described a weird life, be-

Wandering with Wooton

I studied the Bible the other day, and I discovered that the Greek word for "fresh licorice" is used seventeen times to describe heaven! There will be streets of licorice, licorice lakes, and angels whose only job is to hand out licorice.

Okay, I made all of that up, but wouldn't that be *great*? Of course, even better than licorice will be getting to talk to Jesus when He's sitting right in front of me. So cool!

cause she had no concept of what anything looked like. She could feel things like clothes and faces and grass, but she had no idea what colors were. Ginny had no idea what *green* meant. But imagine if there were a miracle, and she was able to see. Suddenly she would be able to understand how wonderful and beautiful the world is. That could be the way it will be when we go to heaven. We can't imagine what pure joy will be like, because we've never felt it. We have no concept of perfection, because we've never seen it. And when we do, we'll see just how wonderful and beautiful heaven is.

Salvation entitles us to the best gift ever: to be with Jesus in heaven for eternity.

Daily Challenge

Draw a picture or describe with words what you think heaven will be like. Then ask your family what they think it will be like.

• • •

Salvation Theme Memory Verse—Ephesians 2:5

[God] gave us new life because of what Christ has done. He gave us life even when we were dead in sin. God's grace has saved you.

Devo
4

And That's Not All!

[Jesus said,] "I have come so they can have life. I want them to have it in the fullest possible way."

It's the offer of the century! For only $19.95, you get a complete fourteen-piece set of steak knives. And these aren't just any knives. These knives can cut through a metal lamppost. And after you're done cutting through a metal lamppost, you can also cut tomatoes in perfect slices. But that's not all! Order now, and you'll also receive a set of forty paring knives. How much would you pay for this? Two hundred dollars? Three hundred? But wait, there's more. . . .

Sounds like a great deal, huh? The offers just don't seem to end.

Salvation gives us a lot more than we think we're getting too. It's easy to concentrate on such a wonderful gift like heaven. But wait, there's more . . .

God also promises Christians a better life here on earth. In John 10:10, Jesus said, "I have come so they can have life. I want them to have it in the fullest possible way." God wants us to have the best life possible. But what does this really mean?

When we are saved, we receive the Holy Spirit. The Holy Spirit is kind of like our conscience. If our minds are telling us to do something that's right, or not to do something that's wrong, that's the Holy Spirit guiding us. He gives us direction. The Holy Spirit also gives us the power to accomplish things we couldn't do on our own.

And that's not all! Galatians 5:22–23 says, "The fruit the Holy Spirit produces is love, joy and peace. It is being patient, kind and good. It is being faithful and gentle and having control of oneself." When we have the Holy Spirit, we're given a huge bucket of these fruits—love, joy, peace, patience, and so on.

Of course, this doesn't mean that once we become Christians our lives are going to

Connie's Corner

One of the first things that Whit said to me after I became a Christian was "Welcome to the family of God." I hadn't really thought about it, but that was really great! I now have a new family. If I have concerns or problems, I can lean on my Christian brothers and sisters–and they can lean on me. That's really important to me. It's just another perk of being a Christian.

be perfect. Being a Christian is hard. Living the way Jesus asks us to is difficult because we want to do things our own way. We want to be selfish. It's our human nature. When we follow Jesus, we put ourselves second. But the rewards far outweigh the tough stuff, don't you think?

And if you get saved in the next thirty seconds, you also get a cheese grater. (Just kidding.)

Daily Challenge

Find eight pieces of fruit at home. Then write the words *love, joy, peace, patience, kindness, faithfulness, gentleness*, and *self-control* on small pieces of paper and label each piece of fruit. (These are the fruits of the Holy Spirit from Galatians 5:22–23.) Every day this week when you eat a piece of fruit, think about the word that's taped to it. For example, if you eat an apple with the word *patience* taped to it, thank God for giving you the Holy Spirit, who helps you to be patient. Then try to be especially patient that day. What a healthy way to remember God's gifts to you!

● ● ●

Salvation Theme Memory Verse—Ephesians 2:5

[God] gave us new life because of what Christ has done. He gave us life even when we were dead in sin. God's grace has saved you.

11

"What Must I Do to Be Saved?"

Today's Verse—Romans 10:9-10

Say with your mouth, "Jesus is Lord." Believe in your heart that God raised him from the dead. Then you will be saved. With your heart you believe and are made right with God. With your mouth you say that Jesus is Lord. And so you are saved.

Eugene Meltsner had come a long way. When he first arrived at Whit's End, he was a scientist first and a human second. Eugene believed that everything could be explained through science. Faith was something people relied on only when they hadn't truly examined the scientific evidence.

But in the *Odyssey* episode "The Time Has Come" (album 25), Eugene came to a crossroads in his life. He had lost a lot of things—Whit's End was closed, Whit had left for the Middle East, and Eugene's girlfriend, Katrina, had broken up with him because she was a Christian and he wasn't.

And possibly worse than anything, he realized that his knowledge was failing him. A spiritual battle was going on around him, and he wasn't equipped to fight it. Evil men had taken over the lives of many people in Odyssey, and Eugene was powerless to stop it.

Jack Allen suggested that Eugene take a look at his life in Odyssey to see what lessons he had learned over the years. So Eugene programmed the Imagination Station to review his past. What he found was the inevitable conclusion: Jesus had been pursuing Eugene for a long time. And Jesus, not Eugene's own intellect, was the One who would save him. He came out of the Imagination Station and asked Jack the question, "What must I do to be saved?"

If you want Jesus in your life, if you believe in your heart that He died for your sins,

Loquacious Learning with Eugene

Did you know that John Newton, the author of the beautiful hymn "Amazing Grace," was at one time a brutal slave trader? But a near-death experience caused John to seek God's mercy and forgiveness. People come to Jesus in many different ways. My wife, Katrina, was informed about Jesus by Connie and Whit, and later that day, she became a Christian. For me, it was a much longer process, but to borrow the colloquialism, "It was worth the wait."

and you want Him to be the Lord of your life right now, the best thing to do is talk to your parents about it. You can also talk to your pastor or a Sunday school teacher.

This is a prayer you can pray together: "Dear Jesus, I know that I sin. And I know that because I sin, I am separated from You and will die one day. But I also know that You died to forgive my sins and take them away forever. Please forgive all my sins right now. I give You my heart, my life, my actions, my attitudes, everything. I want to one day live with You in heaven. Help me to be the follower You want me to be. Amen."

If you prayed that prayer, consider the Bible verse that says "There is joy in heaven over one sinner who turns away from sin" (Luke 15:10). The angels are rejoicing. And you should be too. You've made the best decision you will ever make.

Daily Challenge

Part 1: If you made a decision for Jesus today, tell three adults about it and ask them to pray and celebrate with you. Part 2: Make index cards with one word from the theme verse on each card. Shuffle the cards and then put them in verse order.

• • •

Salvation Theme Memory Verse—Ephesians 2:5

[God] gave us new life because of what Christ has done. He gave us life even when we were dead in sin. God's grace has saved you.

Devo 6

Baptism

Today's Verse—Matthew 3:16

As soon as Jesus was baptized, he came up out of the water.
At that moment heaven was opened. Jesus saw the
Spirit of God coming down on him like a dove.

This was the greatest day ever. This morning as you walked to school, you saved a child's life by pulling him out of the way of an oncoming bus. Then you got an A-plus on a huge biology test even though you studied for only forty-five seconds. Then you were named Student of the Millennium in your school. With the award you were given a brand-new sports car, an all-expenses-paid trip to the moon, and a statue of yourself that will grace the courtyard at your school for all eternity. Then you hit the game-winning home run for your school's baseball team. There happened to be a major-league scout in the stands, and he wants you to be the new cleanup hitter for the New York Yankees. Your starting salary will be eight billion dollars.

What a day! It was so good that you went home that night, sat on your bed, and told . . . no one.

Of course not! If you had a day like that, you would tell everyone! You'd throw a party for six hundred of your closest friends to announce what happened. Right? Well, becoming a Christian is actually way better than all of those things. The statue and the eight billion dollars will fade away some day. But the decision to follow Jesus will mean something for all eternity. So after making such a monumental decision, the first thing you should want to do is to tell people.

This is the purpose of water baptism. It's a public announcement that you are now a follower of Jesus. If you've already asked Jesus into your life, ask your parents or your pastor about getting baptized if you haven't been. There are lots of examples of

Wandering with Wooton

My pastor baptized me in a river in Alaska when I was twelve. It was migrating season for the fish, and just as the pastor was about to dunk me, a fish jumped up into his face. He was so flustered, he said, "This is in honor of your 'salmon' " instead of "salvation." Everyone laughed, but it was okay. I remember the great day when I told everyone I had Jesus in my heart.

baptisms in the Bible. Philip baptized an Ethiopian man (Acts 8). Paul baptized many people, including the jailer who had held him in prison (Acts 16). And before Jesus began His teaching and healing ministry, He was baptized by John in the Jordan River as an example for everyone else (Matthew 3).

Baptism symbolizes the death of your old life and beginning of a new life with Jesus. It's also a picture of how God washes away all of your sin when you're saved. You can start new. Your sins have been forgiven, and your whole life with Christ has begun!

News like that needs to be heard, don't you think?

Daily Challenge

Ask your parents, grandparents, friends, or teachers about their baptism experiences. When and where were they baptized? Who baptized them? Do they remember how they felt?

• • •

Salvation Theme Memory Verse—Ephesians 2:5

[God] gave us new life because of what Christ has done. He gave us life even when we were dead in sin. Gods grace has saved you.

Devo

7

"Okay, I'm Dry. What Now?"

Today's Verse—Luke 2:52

[The boy] Jesus became wiser and stronger. He also became more and more pleasing to God and to people.

Do you ever wonder what happened to Cinderella after the wedding to Prince Charming? Was he a good husband? Did they have children? Did the children get along with their awful aunts and terrible grandmother? How were they able to pay the huge heating bills for that castle? Did Cinderella ever find some sensible shoes that weren't made out of glass?

You may never know, because that part of the story was never written. Your story isn't over once you dry off after getting baptized either. Just because you've given your life to Christ doesn't mean your journey with Jesus is over. It's just beginning. So the question you may be asking now is "What do I do now? Become a missionary to Uzbekicheckiwekistan?"

No. Your first step is to grow in your faith. Learn. Get yourself into good habits like reading your Bible, praying, and having a quiet time with God every day. Reading this devotional book and doing the activities is a great place to start. It's also a good idea to ask lots of questions of people you trust, such as your pastor, your Sunday school teacher, or your parents.

You may be really excited about being a new follower of Jesus. You may want to change the world by immediately becoming a preacher. But all God wants you to do right now is learn.

James 2:26 says, "The body without the spirit is dead. In the same way, faith with-

Whit and Wisdom

In John 3, Jesus talked with a man named Nicodemus. Nicodemus was a religious teacher who wanted to know more about Jesus and His teaching. Jesus talked to him for a while and said some unusual things. For example, Nicodemus was surprised when Jesus told him, "No one can see God's kingdom without being born again" (John 3:3). Nicodemus had no idea what being "born again" meant. Jesus was talking about salvation. Being "born again" means that God takes your old nature–the one you inherited from Adam's sin–and changes it so you'll be a new creature, want to do what's right, and follow Jesus with a clean heart.

out good works is dead." This means that if you have faith but you're not doing the things that help your faith grow, then your faith will die. Your body needs healthy food to grow. In the same way, your faith needs healthy habits to grow. You'll learn a lot more about how to grow in your faith in the section on discipleship.

Your story is just beginning . . .

Family Challenge #1—Tell Your Testimony

At the dinner table this week, ask each person in your family to present his or her "personal testimony"—one person each night. Have family members talk about their journeys of faith, how they first came to know about Jesus, and how they came to realize they needed salvation. If some of your family members aren't followers of Jesus, organize this activity with your friends or a church group.

• • •

Salvation Theme Memory Verse—Ephesians 2:5

[God] gave us new life because of what Christ has done. He gave us life even when we were dead in sin. God's grace has saved you.

Salvation Crossword

Across

1. The least favorite ice-cream flavor at Whit's End. (two words)
4. A word that means "born again."
5. The first name of a religious leader who came to Jesus for answers. (John 3)
8. Wooton's favorite snack.
10. This is a ceremony to publicly announce that you are a Christian.
12. There will be no need for this in heaven, because God is the Light.

Down

2. The Friend who is our conscience.
3. Patience is one of the _____ of the Spirit.
6. Salvation is a _____ from God.
7. The punishment we deserve because of sin.
9. The perfect place.
11. Paul's companion in prison.

Puzzle #1

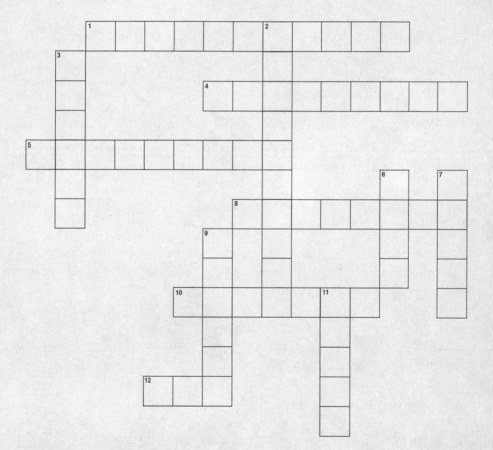

Answers on page 238.

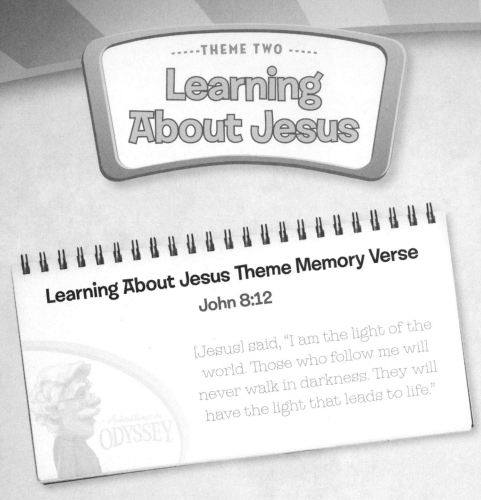

Learning About Jesus

Learning About Jesus Theme Memory Verse
John 8:12

[Jesus] said, "I am the light of the world. Those who follow me will never walk in darkness. They will have the light that leads to life."

Adventures in
ODYSSEY

It's amazing that the God of the universe came down to earth as a human being. Jesus ate lunch, did chores, laughed, and hiccuped—just like you do. But He also calmed storms, healed diseases, performed miracles, and died on a cross, changing the rest of history.

God's Son came into a world darkened by sin, but He didn't leave it that way. He brought life and hope. He gave you an example of how you ought to live as a Christian. In John 8:12, Jesus said, "I am the light of the world. Those who follow me will never walk in darkness. They will have the light that leads to life."

Have you ever gotten up in the middle of the night for a drink of water? When you first turn on the overhead light to find a glass, the light hurts your eyes. You need to cover them to shut out the painful glare.

The people who met Jesus responded like that. They'd been living in darkness, going about things the way they thought best. But when Jesus entered the picture, His "light" was too bright. Some people were drawn to His light, but some people hated Him because of it.

As you read through a few stories about Jesus' life, let Him shine His light on your heart. And choose, even when it isn't comfortable, to follow Him.

Prayer

Dear God,

Thank You for sending Your Son to earth. Help me to learn from the life He lived and also be a light for Jesus in this world.

Amen.

Devo 8

A Not-So-Royal Welcome

Today's Verse—Mark 10:45

Even the Son of Man did not come to be served. Instead, he came to serve others.

Uniformed soldiers rolled out a red carpet. A band stood at attention ready to play. Thousands of people waited outside the gates, jittery with excitement over the king's arrival. Inside, a fancy dinner and big party had been prepared.

That's how a visiting king should be treated. Yet when the King of Kings arrived on earth, He was born in a humble stable. The Lord of the Universe made His appearance, and almost everyone slept through it.

In the *Odyssey* episodes* "Back to Bethlehem, I, II, and III" (album 10), Connie and Eugene took an Imagination Station adventure to witness the birth of Christ. Connie learned that Jesus was actually born in a smelly cave and not a "nice barn" or stable.

God chose a low-key way to introduce His Son to the world. Jesus didn't come to sit in a castle and have people feed Him cupcakes. He came to serve and to love in the humblest of ways.

Do you ever get caught up in what you think you deserve? Maybe you're tired of someone else getting more attention or a bigger piece of cake than you. Or maybe you feel you should have been Student of the Month instead of that boy who always gets his pencil stuck in his ear. Whenever you feel this way, remind yourself that God chose

* To find this episode and the others mentioned in this book, go to *www.whitsend.org/vault*.

Connie's Corner

I was a little miffed that I didn't get a standing ovation after the Christmas play. After all, I wrote the script, painted the backdrop, *and* sprained my ankle chasing the runaway donkey. But then I started to think: If I was really doing all this to honor God, then did it really matter if I was getting praise for myself? I want to live a life that pleases God rather than trying to please everyone else.

for His Son to be born in a sheep's food dish even though Jesus deserved more honor than anyone else. If the King of Kings humbled Himself, you can humble yourself too. And when you do, God will help you love and serve others just like Jesus did!

Daily Challenge

Think of some people you can compliment today. Tell them what you appreciate about them, without expecting anything in return.

• • •

Learning About Jesus Theme Memory Verse—John 8:12

[Jesus] said, "I am the light of the world. Those who follow me will never walk in darkness. They will have the light that leads to life."

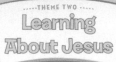
Devo
9

A Holy Lot of Fish and Bread

Today's Verse—Matthew 19:26

With God, all things are possible.

Imagine that you walked into your school cafeteria one day and found out that all the cooks had gone on strike. There was no food—for anyone. Hundreds of kids and teachers with growling stomachs hunted around for food, but they found nothing. And craziest of all, you were the only one who brought lunch that day. A turkey sandwich and an apple. As you unwrapped your sandwich, everyone watched you hungrily. You wondered what to do. You could probably split your lunch with one of your friends, but there would still be a lot more kids who needed something to eat. Now imagine what it would be like if you started dividing up your sandwich and cutting your apple, and the food never ran out! You'd be able to feed the entire school with only your small lunch and still have some left over.

That must have been how the young boy felt in John 6, when Jesus fed a crowd of thousands with only his small lunch of fish and bread.

When you give Jesus something—your time or your talent or your willingness to do something He wants you to do—He can use it to do miraculous things, way beyond what you could do on your own. Sometimes it may be hard to do what God wants you to do. That little boy might have hesitated to hand over his lunch box—he was hungry! But when he gave Jesus his lunch, Jesus used it in a miraculous way.

Is God asking you to do something? Maybe it's talking to an unpopular kid at school, and you feel nervous about it. Or maybe it's giving money to your church. Or

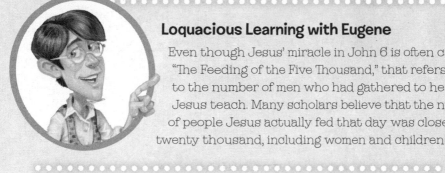

Loquacious Learning with Eugene

Even though Jesus' miracle in John 6 is often called "The Feeding of the Five Thousand," that refers only to the number of men who had gathered to hear Jesus teach. Many scholars believe that the number of people Jesus actually fed that day was closer to twenty thousand, including women and children!

raking the yard of an older neighbor. Whatever it is, God can use even the smallest gift you offer Him and do something amazing with it.

Daily Challenge

Think of a chore you can do for someone or an amount of money you can give to God this week. Tell your family members so they can remind you of your decision.

• • •

Learning About Jesus Theme Memory Verse—John 8:12

[Jesus] said, "I am the light of the world. Those who follow me will never walk in darkness. They will have the light that leads to life."

Devo 10

Going Out on a Limb

Today's Verse—Luke 19:10

The Son of Man came to look
for the lost and save them.

Zach, the shortest kid in eighth grade, sat alone up in the bleachers. No one really liked him, or even noticed him. And the kids at school especially didn't notice him today—not when the school had just won the basketball championship. Zach watched the cheering crowd pour onto the court below. Everyone swarmed around Jesse, who'd scored almost all the points in the game. But then, as Zach watched, it looked as if Jesse was waving at him. What? That didn't make sense. They'd never met. Jesse was popular. Zach was anything but. Suddenly Jesse bounded up the bleacher steps toward the smaller boy. "Hey, Zach! Wanna go to lunch?"

• • •

Let's revisit the two-thousand-year-old version of Zacchaeus's story, which is recorded in Luke 19. It took place during a time when Jesus was pretty popular. You'd think that being so well liked, Jesus would have hung out with people who were really important. But instead, over and over He chose to spend His time with the outcasts of the day—people with diseases, the weak, the unpopular. Even people like Zacchaeus, who sat alone on a tree limb.

Other people weren't happy when Jesus chose to have lunch with Zacchaeus over them. But Jesus told the complainers in Luke 19:10, "The Son of Man came to look for the lost and save them." Jesus didn't come to earth to be popular. He came to love people, especially those no one else did.

Wandering with Wooton

This may surprise you, but I've always been a little strange. I was the only kid at school who packed peanut-butter-and-sardine sandwiches for lunch and had a pet duck named Lois. A lot of kids didn't like me because they thought I was weird. But I always had my friend, Bradford. He reminded me that I was loved and important, even when no one else thought I was. And best of all, Bradford introduced me to Jesus, who changed my life.

Daily Challenge

Think of some people at school or church who don't have a lot of friends. Maybe they're really shy or new or awkward. This week, be friendly with them. Invite one or two to sit with you or share your lunch. Don't worry about what anyone else thinks. Instead, remember how happy it makes God.

• • •

Learning About Jesus Theme Memory Verse—John 8:12

[Jesus] said, "I am the light of the world. Those who follow me will never walk in darkness. They will have the light that leads to life."

Devo
11

Being Sheepish

Today's Verse—John 10:11

[Jesus said,] "I am the good shepherd. The good shepherd gives his life for the sheep."

True or False?
- Former president Woodrow Wilson owned a sheep that chewed tobacco.
- One pound of sheep wool can make ten miles of yarn.
- Sheep are mentioned in the Bible more than any other animal.

Believe it or not, they're all true. And even more significant, Jesus often referred to His followers as sheep, and Himself as a shepherd.

In John 10:11 Jesus said, "I am the good shepherd. The good shepherd gives his life for the sheep." In Jesus' day, sheep were an important part of the culture. Just as we see people walking their dogs today, the people in biblical times saw shepherds leading their flocks of sheep. And people in those days knew what it meant to be a "good shepherd."

A good shepherd in Bible times knew all his sheep. He recognized which ones belonged to him, and he knew each sheep by name. If even one sheep was missing, he'd search long and hard to find it. A good shepherd protected his sheep from wild animals, even if it meant putting himself in danger. He led his sheep to pastures that were safe so the sheep could graze freely. He even nursed sick sheep back to health and bandaged the wounds of any that were injured.

In Bible times, Jesus was a shepherd of people. He taught them, guided them, and cared for them. If you belong to Jesus, He is your "Good Shepherd" too. He knows you by name and watches over you. He cares deeply for you and wants to lead you to safe places where you can grow. Jesus is a shepherd you can trust.

Loquacious Learning with Eugene

Do you know that if a sheep tips over on its back, it can't get up because of the weight of its wool? If left alone, it could actually die. A shepherd must be nearby to help the sheep get back on its feet, often using the crook of his staff. Indeed, sheep very much need their shepherds.

Daily Challenge

Look up Psalm 23 and read it. Pay special attention to the parts about the Lord as your Shepherd. Write down all the ways He "shepherds" you.

• • •

Learning About Jesus Theme Memory Verse—John 8:12

[Jesus] said, "I am the light of the world. Those who follow me will never walk in darkness. They will have the light that leads to life."

Devo 12

The Rest of the Time

Today's Verse—Psalm 46:10

Be still, and know that I am God.

"I need a break!"

How many times have you said this? Whether it's during a long study session, after a tough basketball practice, or when your little sister is driving you crazy, sometimes you just need to get away.

Do you know Jesus needed to take a break too? Several times in the Bible, it's mentioned that Jesus often took breaks from teaching the crowds of people. He would go off alone and find a quiet place to spend time with His Father. Even when He was twelve years old, He went to the temple on His own to spend time with the priests in His Father's house. He longed to be with God.

It can be easy to get so busy—even with good things—that we don't take time simply to sit with God. We might listen to a Bible story at church or do a missions project, but we can sometimes neglect just "being" with God. He wants us to spend time alone with Him, telling Him about the things that hurt us or that we're afraid of. He wants us to listen to Him as we read through the Bible and thank Him for the ways He's blessed us.

It's in the quiet that God can impress things on our hearts. Psalm 46:10 says, "Be still, and know that I am God." Jesus recognized that for Him to do His ministry well, He needed that time with God—and so do each of us!

Daily Challenge

Set aside some time to take a walk with God—just you and Him. Admire His creation. Tell Him what you're afraid of or excited about. Thank Him for caring about you so much that He wants to spend time with you.

Wandering with Wooton

While I was painting 74,324 paper cups brick brown for my Tower of Babel Sunday school lesson, I realized I needed to make lemonade. (Because looking at all these cups would make anyone thirsty.) And since I was going to make lemonade, I realized I should probably bake a few loaves of licorice banana bread to go with it. It took a long time to get ready for Sunday school. And I was so busy getting stuff done that I forgot to spend time with God. But I need Him way more than I need paper cups!

• • •

Learning About Jesus Theme Memory Verse—John 8:12

[Jesus] said, "I am the light of the world. Those who follow me will never walk in darkness. They will have the light that leads to life."

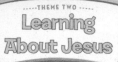

THEME TWO
Learning About Jesus

Devo 13

Doing the Unexpected

Today's Verse—John 11:25

[Jesus said,] "I am the resurrection and the life."

Can you imagine having Jesus over for a birthday party? Or going on a camping trip with Him? You might not often think of Jesus hanging out with His friends, but He had a lot of them. One of His good friends was Lazarus, and Lazarus's two sisters, Mary and Martha.

One day, Lazarus became very sick. Mary rushed a message to Jesus asking Him to come—*now!* But Jesus waited three days before He came. And by the time He strolled into Mary and Martha's neighborhood, Lazarus was dead and buried.

"Lord, I wish you had been here," Mary said when she saw Him. "Then my brother would not have died." (For the whole story, read John 11.)

Have you ever felt that way? Maybe sometimes you wonder if Jesus knows what's going on in your life, or if He even cares. You might be praying for something, but it doesn't seem as if Jesus is even listening. That's how Mary felt.

But then, amazingly, in front of a shocked crowd, Jesus called Lazarus out of his tomb. And, still wrapped in grave clothes, Lazarus emerged, as alive as ever!

God never forgets about you. He has an even bigger plan for you than you have for yourself. And He loves surprising you with unexpected blessings. Even when He doesn't answer your prayers as you hope, you can trust that He is working out His plan for you. He created you for a purpose (Ephesians 2:10), He hears your prayers (1 John 5:14–15), and He thinks of you often (Psalm 139:17).

Connie's Corner

I really prayed hard that God would help things work out with this guy I liked, Mitch. Then when they didn't, I wondered if God even cared about me. But later I realized it was for the best, and I was so thankful things didn't work out with Mitch. God knows what He's doing w-a-a-a-y more than I do. Go figure.

Daily Challenge

Write down all your concerns and worries on a piece of paper and pray over them, thanking God that He's in control of each one. At the top of the page, write in marker, "God's got a plan." Put the paper somewhere to remind yourself that God is always at work.

• • •

Learning About Jesus Theme Memory Verse—John 8:12

[Jesus] said, "I am the light of the world. Those who follow me will never walk in darkness. They will have the light that leads to life."

Devo
14

Hope Returned

● ●

Today's Verse—John 3:16

God loved the world so much that he gave his one and only Son.
Anyone who believes in him will not die but will have eternal life.

● ●

In the *Odyssey* episodes "The Imagination Station, I and II" (album 5), Digger
Digwillow was transported via one of Whit's inventions to the day when Jesus
was put to death. Digger saw Jesus being unjustly beaten, whipped, mocked, and
hung on a cross to die. The scene brought Digger to tears.

But God had bigger plans than the disciples (or Digger) could imagine. "God
loved the world so much that he gave his one and only Son. Anyone who believes in
him will not die but will have eternal life" (John 3:16).

And on the third day after His death, Jesus emerged from the tomb. The disciples
couldn't even believe it at first. They'd given up. Some had left town. One had denied
even knowing Him. But hope had returned, bigger and better than ever.

God's plan wasn't about conquering the Roman Empire. It was all about redeem-
ing the world and giving us the opportunity to live with Him forever.

Daily Challenge

Journal about the time you accepted the Lord as your Savior, and share what you write
with a friend. If you've never asked Jesus into your life, talk to your parents or pastor
about how you can do this.

Family Challenge #2—Parable Charades

Write down the following Scripture references on separate scraps of paper: Matthew
7:24–27 (The Wise and Foolish Builders); Matthew 18:10–14 (The Lost Sheep);

Whit and Wisdom

At Whit's End the other day, one of the kids asked me, "Why did Jesus have to die?" I thought it was a great question. I explained that God is perfect and holy and when Adam and Eve sinned in the garden of Eden, they separated all of humanity from Him (Isaiah 59:2). They also introduced death into the world.

For thousands of years, the only way people could connect with God was through the death of specially chosen animals who would spill their blood as a payment for their sins (Hebrews 10: 1-2). But God knew that the only way to destroy the power of sin and death in mankind was to offer the perfect sacrifice: His only Son Jesus (John 3:16). Jesus was perfect and holy, and His death covered all of our sins. More than that, Jesus rose again from the dead three days later, proving that He was more powerful than our sins, than evil, even death itself. Because of Jesus, we can have new life. And the power of sin no longer holds us in its death-grip. In fact, we're dead to sin! (Ephesians 2:1-6). That's just one reason why they call the gospel the "good news!"

Matthew 20:1–16 (The Workers in the Vineyard); Mark 4:3–9 (The Sower); Luke 10:30–37 (The Good Samaritan); Luke 14:7–14 (The Wedding Feast); Luke 15:8–10 (The Lost Coin); Luke 15:11–32 (The Prodigal Son).

Then divide your family into teams. Each team secretly selects a "parable passage," checks the Bible, and acts out the parable. See if other family members can guess which parable you're reenacting. Then talk about it. What does this parable tell you about God's character? In what way does it encourage you?

• • •

Learning About Jesus Theme Memory Verse—John 8:12

[Jesus] said, "I am the light of the world. Those who follow me will never walk in darkness. They will have the light that leads to life."

35

Jesus' Character Word Search

Circle the words below that describe Jesus.
To check your answers, find the words in the grid.

MIRACLE-WORKER

WEALTHY

PLUMBER

COMPASSIONATE

HUMBLE

VIOLENT

SACRIFICING

SHEPHERD

STORYTELLER

HATEFUL

HANDSOME

LIGHT

ALIVE

SELFISH

REDEEMER

IRISH

FASHIONABLE

LOVING

HYPOCRITE

FORGIVING

ARROGANT

SINLESS

MERCIFUL

POLITICIAN

LACTOSE-INTOLERANT

```
M I R A C L E W O R K E R E R A B Z T R
W D E Y O I U I V J F W O R L G C E
H S A C M G R L R O F M S T N N O D
O L O V P H E E P S I Q H I R H M E
S L A L A T L D I L I L V F O U P E
H L O C S O T M M E R I M O T S S M
E I I V S C H S E T G O I R S T I E
S G C G I I G R C R C O R S H O N R
A O S O O N E A O E C A L I L R T T
C F T T N M G F L M M I I S O Y F O
R O S O A R G I V E E I F R V T O T
I R A L T M S H U E R G H U O E G H
F G S H E P H E R D S M E R L L I O
I M I R L I U M E E E A P L T L Z T
C S H C A L M I O R R S I N L E S S
I H A R E M B R R E D E N R E R U H
N S V I L A L I V E R M I R L O V M
G W O R K S E H U M E R C C R E M L
```

Answers on page 238.

Discipleship

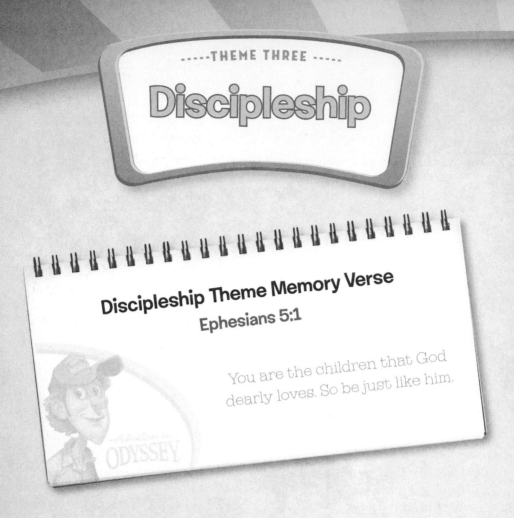

Discipleship Theme Memory Verse
Ephesians 5:1

You are the children that God dearly loves. So be just like him.

Adventures in ODYSSEY

It's the darkest of nights. You're in a boat with friends. The wind is howling. Waves splash over the sides of the boat. Something ghostly comes toward you on the water. You shiver, terrified. There's nowhere to hide.

"Don't worry! It's me," a familiar voice cries.

"If it's you, then tell me to come," says your friend Peter.

"Come."

Suddenly Peter leaps out of the boat . . .

• • •

If someone did that today, you'd probably be fishing him out of the lake. But the apostle Peter actually walked on water! He loved and trusted Jesus so much, he wanted to copy Him, even if it meant stepping out of a boat onto waves. As long as Peter trusted Jesus, he stayed on top of the water. But when Peter took his eyes off Jesus, fearing the wind and the waves, he sank, and Jesus had to rescue him. (You can read the whole story in Matthew 14:25–32.)

Peter's experience was like discipleship. *Discipleship* means deciding *on purpose* to grow in your faith and do everything you can to become more like Jesus.

What does it take to be a disciple of Jesus? Why should you want to be? What happens if you try and fail?

This week you'll discover how to be a true disciple of Jesus. Don't be surprised if it feels like a stormy boat ride. Discipleship has ups and downs, but Jesus can keep you on top of the waves.

Prayer

Dear God,

This week teach me how to become more like Jesus. Help me want that more than anything else, and remind me to depend on You to make it happen. In Jesus' name.

Amen.

Devo
15

Just Like Whit

Today's Verse—2 Corinthians 3:18

Our faces are not covered with a veil. We all display
the Lord's glory. We are being changed to become
more like him so that we have more and more glory.
And the glory comes from the Lord, who is the Holy Spirit.

How would you like to run Whit's End for a weekend? Connie and Eugene got that chance in the *Odyssey* episode* "Let This Mind Be in You" (album 4).

Connie was afraid she'd mess up, but Whit said to just do things the way he would. So Connie wore a sweater like Whit's. She figured she'd act more like Whit if she dressed like him. When Jack and Lucy came in with a Bible question, Connie answered them just as Whit would—by telling a story. Only she couldn't quite remember the facts.

Next, Jennifer needed her. The Bible Verse Mirror kept repeating the same words. Connie tried turning the mirror off. But it just said the words faster. She pulled out a wire. The mirror went crazy.

"Connie, make it stop!" Jennifer cried.

Connie hit the mirror over and over. "I . . . want . . . you . . . to . . . stop!"

Crash. It stopped.

Then Jimmy Barclay needed advice. Connie thought Whit would be proud of how she'd helped Jimmy. But the next day Jimmy's dad complained about the bad advice she had given.

Connie was ready to quit. She told Eugene, "I can't do *anything* like Mr. Whittaker!"

---

* Want more episodes on the same theme? Visit *www.whitsend.org/vault* and browse by lesson.

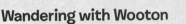

Wandering with Wooton

I've been thinking about copycats. A copy machine could copy a cat. A cat who could make copies for me would be really helpful. But usually, people don't like copycats. They're annoying 'cause they just copy everything. In some ways, though, I should be a copycat, if the person I'm copying is Jesus. I want to still be the unique person I am, but more like Jesus every day.

Eugene concluded that Connie had misunderstood Whit's instructions. He said, "Whit didn't say to *be* him. He said to be *like* him."

Connie realized she needed to do the things Whit taught her while still being herself.

Jesus said, "Be perfect, just as your Father in heaven is perfect" (Matthew 5:48). It takes a lifetime of following Jesus to become like Him. God will make you perfect in heaven. Until then, with His help, you can grow more like Jesus every day. God didn't make you to *be* Jesus. He made you to be just who you are—and to be *like* Jesus in the way you live.

Daily Challenge

Write down all the good things about Jesus that you would like to imitate. Ask God to help you become like Jesus in these ways.

• • •

Discipleship Theme Memory Verse—Ephesians 5:1

You are the children that God dearly loves. So be just like him.

Devo 16

Try, Try Again

Today's Verse—2 Timothy 1:7

God didn't give us a spirit that makes us weak and fearful. He gave us a spirit that gives us power and love. It helps us control ourselves.

Have you ever tried to do something over and over and failed? How would you like to try and fail for more than twenty years?

That happened to William Wilberforce. He lived in England from 1759 to 1833 and was a member of the British Parliament. When he was about twenty-five years old, Wilberforce became a believer in Jesus Christ. Three years later, he realized that God was calling him to help end the slave trade in England. At that time, English slave traders kidnapped men, women, and children from their homes in Africa. These Africans were transported in ships to places around the world where they would become slaves.

Wilberforce and his friends learned about the terrible way the traders and buyers treated the Africans. The English traders considered the Africans their property. Wilberforce and the other abolitionists (those who wanted to end slavery) knew the slaves were people just like them.

Over and over, Wilberforce tried to get British lawmakers to vote to end the slave trade. Sometimes they criticized him. Sometimes they ignored him. Often they laughed at him. After years of trying and failing, Wilberforce finally witnessed the vote in Parliament that ended the slave trade, and he cried.

Wilberforce kept fighting, but it was thirty-six more years before the English did away with slavery completely. Three days before he died, Wilberforce heard that slavery in the British Empire would finally come to an end.

Wilberforce got discouraged, but he never gave up. Trying to become more like

Connie's Corner

Boy, I sure know what it's like to fail. It seems I'm always messing up. Like the time I broke the Bible Verse Mirror. And it doesn't help when your boss is the most perfect man alive—Mr. Whittaker. But one of the things that makes Whit so good is that he's so patient with me. Just like God is. I'm glad God loves me the way I am. It makes me want to be more like Him.

Jesus can also be discouraging. In the *Odyssey* episode "Do, for a Change" (album 26), Zachary tried to act like a Christian, but he kept failing. He lost his temper and kept getting into trouble. He almost quit. Then Jack Allen told him that all Christians struggle with sin, but they shouldn't give up trying to be holy. Jack explained that it would be like giving up baths because you're just going to get dirty again. God gives all Christians grace. God forgives them and gives everyone a chance to start over.

Daily Challenge

Take a wad of paper and stand a few feet away from a trash can. Think of one way you're having trouble being like Jesus. Maybe it's your temper, your words, or your attitude. Maybe you cheat on tests or lie to your parents. Think of that thing as you throw the paper into the trash. Move farther back and do it again and again until the paper goes in every time. Remember, the more you try to be like Jesus with God's help, the better you'll do.

• • •

Discipleship Theme Memory Verse—Ephesians 5:1

You are the children that God dearly loves. So be just like him.

Devo 17

Stand Strong

Today's Verse—1 Corinthians 16:13–14

Be on your guard. Stand firm in the faith.
Be brave. Be strong. Be loving in everything you do.

"The Canaanites are too strong for us!" the Israelite scouts said. "Their cities have high walls."

Caleb disagreed with the other scouts. God had told them to conquer the Canaanites. God had promised that land to the Israelites.

Caleb shouted to the others, "We certainly *can* do it. Let's go and get them!"

"Are you kidding?" said one of the scouts who had also spied out the land with Caleb. "The Canaanites are as large as giants. We're like grasshoppers compared to them. They'll eat us alive!"

The people of Israel wailed. They had expected to enter the Promised Land, but now it looked impossible.

"Why did we trust Moses and Aaron?" they said. "Those people will kill us and take our families! We should pick another leader and go back to Egypt."

Moses and Aaron fell facedown on the ground in sadness.

Joshua, who had also seen the land, stood with Caleb. Joshua and Caleb tore their clothes to show their grief. They said, "It's a good land. Why should we be afraid? Those people have no protection. We have the Lord. Don't rebel against Him!"

The Israelites wanted to stone Caleb and Joshua for their words. But God rewarded these men for their faithfulness. He let them enter the Promised Land forty years later. The other adults of that time died in the desert. (See Numbers 13–14.)

Sometimes as a disciple of Jesus, you will have to take a stand as did Joshua and Caleb. You might even have to stand alone. God will reward your faithfulness. It's

Loquacious Learning with Eugene

If only the Israelites fully understood the Universal Law of Patterns as do you and I! It was illogical for the Israelites to cower in the face of obstacles. God had delivered them from the Egyptians with plagues and fire. He had escorted them through the desert and had made a path for them through the Red Sea on dry land! By scientific reasoning, why didn't the Israelites believe He would do it again? I must conclude, then, that the Israelites suffered from obstinacy. Then again, don't we all?

important to remain faithful to Jesus, because He is the way, the truth, and the life. He is the only way for people to enter the Promised Land of heaven. (See John 14:6.)

Others need to see Jesus through you. That's why you need to become more like Him every day. Do your very best to obey Him and stand strong. And no matter how big or scary others may seem, remember that God is infinitely greater.

Daily Challenge

Write out today's verse on a piece of paper. Decorate the page with pictures of how you can stand strong for Jesus. Post it where you can see it. Each day this week, ask the Lord to build up your faith in Him and help you stand strong, no matter who disagrees with you.

• • •

Discipleship Theme Memory Verse—Ephesians 5:1

You are the children that God dearly loves. So be just like him.

Devo 18

Everything for Jesus

Today's Verse—Matthew 16:24

Then Jesus spoke to his disciples. He said, "If anyone wants to follow me, he must say no to himself. He must pick up his cross and follow me."

Imagine that your dad and uncle own a restaurant. One day you're helping them after school, wiping tables. Suddenly a man walks in. He tells your dad and uncle, "Follow me. I'll make you more successful than you ever dreamed. You can learn to feed people without giving them food."

Without a word to you or the other employees, your dad and uncle remove their aprons and leave with the man. You run outside and see the stranger enter the restaurant across the street. A father and two brothers own it. The brothers leave their father at the door and follow the stranger down the street.

Something very similar happened in the Bible. When Jesus saw Peter and Andrew with their fishing nets, He said to them, "Come. Follow me. I will make you fishers of people" (Matthew 4:19). Peter and Andrew left at once to follow Jesus.

Then Jesus called out to James and John, who were working on the family fishing boat. The men immediately left their father, Zebedee, and followed him.

True disciples of Jesus are willing to give up everything for Him and do whatever He asks. The joy, love, and peace He offers more than make up for anything we give up to serve Him.

Jesus said, "Has anyone left home or family for God's kingdom? They will receive many times as much in this world. In the world to come they will live forever" (Luke 18:29–30).

Now that's a reward worth everything!

Connie's Corner

I get kind of scared thinking about what God might ask me to do. I mean, will He send me off to some dark, snake-infested rain forest to tell the natives about Jesus? Then I remember how much He loves me. After what Jesus did on the cross for me, I should probably be able to deal with a few snakes or piranha... Okay, maybe just the snakes. Besides, the Bible says I can do everything by His power (Philippians 4:13). And you know what? I believe it.

• • •

In the *Odyssey* episode "The Secret Keys of Discipline" (album 20), Danny Schmidt wanted to play the piano in a talent show. But he kept skipping practice when his friends urged him to do other things. Danny learned to say no to his friends and yes to keeping his commitments. Then he was rewarded for his hard work.

God may ask you to do things you don't want to do. If you learn to say no to self and yes to Him, you'll receive joy, and He'll receive the glory He deserves.

Daily Challenge

Pray about ways you can say no to yourself and yes to God this week. Ask Him to show you what good works you can do to serve Him and others. (Did you know you were created to do good works? See Ephesians 2:10.) Do at least one hard thing each day to feel the joy of pleasing Him.

• • •

Discipleship Theme Memory Verse—Ephesians 5:1

You are the children that God dearly loves. So be just like him.

Devo 19

Different for Jesus

Today's Verse—1 Peter 1:14–15

You should obey. You shouldn't give in to evil longings. They controlled your life when you didn't know any better. The one who chose you is holy. So you should be holy in all that you do.

In devotion 18, we talked about Danny Schmidt who learned to say no to himself and yes to God. In the *Odyssey* episode "All the Difference in the World" (album 23), Danny Schmidt didn't like his life. Not since he'd spent the night with Jeff. Jeff's family had just moved to Odyssey.

Jeff gets to do anything he wants, Danny complained to himself. *My parents don't let me have any fun. Why do I have to be different?*

Danny figured he'd seem like a weirdo if he didn't like the same movies and music as other kids. So he listened to loud music and watched scary shows. He stopped praying and started talking back to his parents. It didn't go over so well. He got sent to his room.

Even a talk with his dad didn't change Danny's mind. He simply didn't want to be different anymore. He proved it the next weekend at Jeff's house. He disobeyed his parents and convinced Jeff to watch a movie both sets of parents had forbidden. In the middle of the movie, Jeff's parents came home.

Danny knew he was in trouble, but he didn't realize how much damage he'd done. No one in Jeff's family was a Christian. The Schmidts had been telling Jeff's parents about the wonderful difference Jesus makes in people's lives. But Danny's disobedience made Christians, and especially Jesus, look bad. Danny was sorry. He realized he needed to be different because he believed in Jesus.

Jeff and his family became Christians anyway, and they soon found out that Jesus does make a difference—all the difference in the world.

Wandering with Wooton

People say I'm different from other people. I'm sort of proud of that. For instance, it's fabulous the way words simply flow from my brain. Watch this. Flow . . . flap . . . floss . . . Dental floss cuts cake into perfect slices. Life is sweeter with cake. And even sweeter with Jesus. There! I did it! I made a point! My mind works weird like that. With Jesus, it's okay to be different. But I've been thinking I'll try to be more the same from now on. The same as Jesus.

It's okay to be different. In fact, if you love Jesus, it's absolutely necessary. Romans 12:2 says, "Don't live any longer the way this world lives. Let your way of thinking be completely changed. Then you will be able to test what God wants for you. And you will agree that what he wants is right. His plan is good and pleasing and perfect."

Daily Challenge

Make a disciple acrostic out of the word *psalm*. P could stand for "Pray always." What would S stand for? Write the acrostic on a piece of paper. Then hang it where you'll see it and be reminded of what a good disciple of Jesus should do.

• • •

Discipleship Theme Memory Verse—Ephesians 5:1

You are the children that God dearly loves. So be just like him.

Devo 20

Even the Greatest Obeyed

Today's Verse—2 Corinthians 10:5

I keep every thought under control in order to make it obey Christ.

In the *Odyssey* episode "The Fundamentals" (album 21), Phil McFarland thought he knew everything about playing basketball. He wouldn't let the coach correct his shooting style. Then Phil played against Rusty Gordon, who blocked all of Phil's shots. Finally, Phil asked for help and learned to become a better player.

When we obey God and take correction from those who are wiser in His ways than we are, we become better disciples of Jesus. Our lives honor Him, and everyone's a lot better off.

Even Jesus, the greatest of all, was obedient when He lived on earth. Just think about how wise and powerful He is! He's the Word of God who created the universe (John 1:1–3). He did so many wonderful things while He was here that John said the whole world couldn't hold enough books to tell about them all (John 21:25). That's some power! Almighty power! Awesome power!

But even though He had all that power, Jesus still obeyed His parents. Remember when He was twelve? Mary and Joseph found Him in the temple talking with the Jewish teachers. Jesus wanted to be in His Father's house, but He returned to Nazareth when His parents asked Him to (Luke 2:41–52).

More important, Jesus, who is God the Son, obeyed God the Father. That meant dying for our sins on the cross. In the garden of Gethsemane, Jesus prayed, "My Father, if it is possible, take this cup of suffering away from me. But let what you want be done,

Loquacious Learning with Eugene

Temperance, or mastering our desires, is a trait I admire. In Galatians 5, the apostle Paul named temperance as one of the fruits of the Spirit. Temperance comes from the Greek word *enkrateia*, often translated "self-control." This implies more than controlling ourselves. It means we must allow the Holy Spirit to control us, because even disciplined human beings like myself often fail in the attempt.

not what I want" (Matthew 26:39). He was willing to obey His Father even if it meant dying on a cross!

Being a disciple of Jesus means becoming like Him in obedience. Jesus said, "If you love me, you will obey what I command" (John 14:15). If you trust that God loves you and knows what He's doing, you'll honor Him by obeying His Word. You'll also obey the people He has placed in authority over you, especially your parents.

Jesus, the greatest of all, obeyed. And now you have the joy of obeying Him.

Daily Challenge

Think about one way you could learn to obey God more completely. Talk with your parents about it. Ask them for advice on how to obey better. Ask God to help you improve in this area. At the end of the week, talk with your parents again and see how well you did.

• • •

Discipleship Theme Memory Verse—Ephesians 5:1

You are the children that God dearly loves. So be just like him.

Devo 21

Jesus, Not Me

Today's Verse—1 Peter 5:6

Don't be proud. Put yourselves under God's mighty hand. Then he will honor you at the right time.

Have you ever heard of making paper from peanuts? Or dye and paste from sweet potatoes? Would you like to serve peanut punch at your next party? Because of a man named George, you could have—if you had his recipes.

When George was a child, flowers and plants amazed him. He painted, grew, collected, and studied them. George became a Christian at age ten and grew in his faith until he died.

During his life, George made many scientific discoveries. He helped Southern farmers learn to protect their soil by rotating their crops. He taught them to grow sweet potatoes, soybeans, peas, peanuts, and pecans, instead of just cotton. Then he found hundreds of ways to use those crops.

This man with so many brilliant ideas was George Washington Carver. He was born a slave and grew to become a great man of God. He wasn't great because he worked hard to get an education and did so many wonderful things. He was great because he was humble. He knew his talents came from God, and he used them to help others.

It's the same for us. We need to remember that everything we are is all because of Jesus. "Every good and perfect gift is from God" (James 1:17).

Family Challenge #3—Ice-Cream Social

Plan a fun evening with your parents and siblings. Gather your favorite ice-cream flavors and toppings and make sundaes together. While you're eating them, talk about some of the good times you've had together. Then share what each of you thinks was

Whit and Wisdom

Y'know, some people think it's wrong to admit our strengths. They think we should pretend we don't have the talents or gifts that we have in order to look "humble." The truth is, pretending like that is really a "false humility" because it denies what God has given to us. <u>True</u> humility comes from understanding that our gifts and strengths come from God. We don't deserve them. We didn't earn them. But we have them to use for God and His Kingdom. Philippians 2:13 tells us that God helps us *want* to do His will and *act* according to His good purposes.

That's what discipleship is all about. As followers of Jesus, we surrender ourselves to God every day and try to become more like Jesus. God wouldn't tell us to be like Jesus without giving us the strength and ability to do it.

The apostle Paul wrote, "My God will meet all your needs. He will meet them in keeping with his wonderful riches that come to you because you belong to Christ Jesus" (Philippians 4:19). The Bible and prayer give us a clue as to what God wants in our lives. Then He helps us to trust and obey Him—and to use our talents for Him. Then, when we succeed, we can give Him the praise and thanks He deserves for working through us.

the best time you've spent together and why. Ask family members to explain why they thought some activities were better than others.

Next talk about some of the things Jesus did during His life on earth. Jesus always chose the best things to do. Discuss how you can follow Jesus by trying to choose the best things from the many good choices available. The following Discipleship Quiz will give you some ideas to get started.

• • •

Discipleship Theme Memory Verse—Ephesians 5:1

You are the children that God dearly loves. So be just like him.

Puzzle #3

Discipleship Quiz

Read the scenes below and then follow these directions:

1. Choose the child who *best* shows Christian discipleship described in the verse following each scene.
2. Discuss the possible answers as a family.
3. Look up the Scripture verse at the end of the scene and discuss it. It gives a clue to the answer.
4. Write the first initial of your answer in the blanks following the last scene.
5. Unscramble the letters to discover a message about living for Jesus Christ.

SCENE 1: Anna, Ella, and Olivia liked Sunday school. Anna always brought her Bible. Ella raised her hand to answer questions. Olivia always knew the memory verse. (Psalm 119:11)

SCENE 2: Wade, Gabe, and Jackson found out that Chase, a boy in their class, didn't know Jesus. Wade ate lunch with Chase every day and told him about Jesus. Gabe gave him a tract. Jackson invited him to church. (Luke 5:29–32)

SCENE 3: Frank, Kayleigh, and Grace all hurt Dylan's feelings. Frank admitted he was wrong and asked Dylan to forgive him. Kayleigh explained why she said what she did and added, "I'm sorry you misunderstood me." Grace said, "Sorry," as she handed Dylan a cookie from her lunch. (Proverbs 28:13)

SCENE 4: Megan, Whitney, and Lacey all wanted to go on a field trip that cost twenty dollars. Megan saved it from her allowance. Whitney asked her parents for the money. Lacey did extra chores

and gave up snacks for two weeks to earn the money, but then she decided to give the money away. (Matthew 16:24)

SCENE 5: A new family moved into the neighborhood. Ethan mowed and trimmed the new family's lawn the morning they moved in. Uri told them about the best pizza places. Aiden waved every time he saw them. (Ephesians 5:2)

SCENE 6: Carson, Matt, Owen, and Joshua went fishing. Carson's reel broke. Matt said he was sorry it happened. Owen let Carson use his pole and looked for worms instead of fishing. Joshua gave Carson one of the fish he caught. (Luke 6:31)

SCENE 7: Isabella, Ben, and Logan represented their school in a state science fair. Isabella kept their display neat. Ben talked respectfully to the judges. Logan told everyone about the good work Isabella and Ben had done on their project. (Philippians 2:3)

SCENE 8: Sophie, Noah, and Madeline wanted to surprise their mother. She would be gone for the two hours when they usually did their chores. Sophie made her mom's favorite dessert. Noah made her a fancy card. Madeline did her chores and then cut flowers to make a bouquet, but her mom got home before she finished. (1 Samuel 15:22)

Initials: 1. ___ 2. ___ 3. ___ 4. ___ 5. ___ 6. ___ 7. ___ 8. ___

Now, unscramble those eight letters to find

a two-word message about discipleship:

___ ___ ___ ___ ___ ___   ___ ___.

Answers on page 239.

Prayer

Prayer Theme Memory Verse
1 Thessalonians 5:17

Never stop praying.

ODYSSEY

Prayer happens all over the place. We pray three or four times during church. We pray before meals. We attend prayer meetings. There's a prayer chapel at the hospital. We see football players kneel down and pray after a touchdown. There's a National Day of Prayer in May. Prayers are written on posters, crocheted into blankets, painted on dishes. There are prayer chains, prayer cloths, prayer beads, prayer books, prayer groups, prayer guides, prayer journals, prayer requests, and prayer vigils. Even sticks of gum have prayers written across them! All of this makes us wonder . . .

"What are all these people praying about?"

Actually, there is plenty to pray about. As we'll find out this week, we should pray to God about *everything*. There are a kabillion things we need to thank God for and confess to Him. There are many requests, for ourselves and for others, that God wants us to bring to Him.

In 1855, Joseph M. Scriven wrote a hymn called "What a Friend We Have in Jesus." The first verse goes like this:

What a Friend we have in Jesus, all our sins and griefs to bear!
What a privilege to carry everything to God in prayer!
O what peace we often forfeit, O what needless pain we bear,
All because we do not carry everything to God in prayer.

When it comes right down to it, maybe there's not *enough* prayer. So let's all get on our knees!

But before we do that, could I bother you for some prayer gum?

Prayer

Lord,

Teach me to pray. Help me to be honest, grateful, and pure of heart when I come before You this week.

Amen.

Devo
22

The Best Friend

Today's Verse—Psalm 5:3

Lord, in the morning you hear my voice. In the
morning I pray to you. I wait for you in hope.

Jeff and Drew grew up together as next-door neighbors. Their houses were close
enough for them to talk on walkie-talkies at night before bed. They played and
talked and were the best of friends. As teenagers they listened to music together, pigged
out on pizza on the back porch, and shared their dreams.

Jeff loved Drew with all of his heart. Drew was a great friend to have. Drew listened
to everything Jeff told him. Whenever Jeff followed Drew's advice, everything would
work out. Drew laughed when Jeff was happy and cried when Jeff was sad. Immediately
after talking to Drew, Jeff would feel stronger. He would feel as if he could do anything.

High school graduation came, and Jeff and Drew went separate ways. At first Jeff
called Drew every day. But after a while, Jeff got distracted with college life, and the
conversations between Jeff and Drew happened less frequently. By the time Jeff gradu-
ated from college, he barely talked to Drew at all.

Then Jeff's life started to change. He no longer had the great advice giver around
him. He began to make decisions on his own. He took a job he shouldn't have taken,
and he was miserable. He moved to a big city and felt lonely.

Then Jeff was fired from his job. He had no friends and had nowhere to turn.
Finally, with tears in his eyes, he picked up the phone. He was certain that Drew was
angry with him for never calling.

Drew answered. "Hello, Jeff. It's so good to hear from you!" Drew was willing and
ready to be Jeff's friend.

• • •

Connie's Corner

I set my alarm for 6:15 every morning. On good days I get up, pray for ten minutes, shower, eat breakfast, and head out the door. But some days I hit the Snooze button, sleep until 6:24, and then pray for one minute, shower, breakfast, and head out the door. On bad days I hit the Snooze button four times, get up at 6:51, skip everything, and head out the door. When I skip praying, I always feel yucky all day. Praying gets my head right.

And this is how it is with prayer. We have a friend near us at all times—God. He will always listen. He has great advice for us. He has the power to help us in any situation. And yet, how often do we forget that He's there to talk to! We get busy with our lives, and we ignore the One who can make a difference in us.

Don't lose touch with the best Friend we could ever have.

Daily Challenge

Find a small sticker and put it on your watch or on the back of your hand (anywhere it won't fall off). Every time you look down and see the sticker today, say a short prayer. It can be about anything. Just talk to God, and He will be listening.

• • •

Prayer Theme Memory Verse—1 Thessalonians 5:17

Never stop praying.

Devo 23

How to Pray, Part I: Thanksgiving and Praise

Today's Verse—Psalm 100:4

Give thanks as you enter the gates of [God's] temple. Give praise as you enter its courtyards. Give thanks to him and praise his name.

Have you ever tried to cook or bake something by following a recipe? Can you imagine a recipe like this?

Spinach and Cheese Soufflé
Step one: Make a soufflé.
Step two: Add spinach.
Step three: Add cheese.

That wouldn't be very helpful, would it? The recipe writer assumed the reader already knows how to make a soufflé! The Bible talks about prayer a lot, and Jesus wanted us to know how to pray. He understood that it wasn't good enough to just tell us to pray without showing us how to do it. So He gave us a demonstration.

Luke 11:2 is the Lord's Prayer, which starts out "Father, may your name be honored." In Jesus' example, He started His prayer with honoring God. This is what praise is. Your prayers don't have to be in any particular order, but it sometimes helps, right at the beginning, to acknowledge whom you're praying to. A good way to do that is to honor God with praise and thanksgiving. *Praise* is honoring God for who He is. *Thanksgiving* is honoring God for what He has done.

Wandering with Wooton

I used to write down things I was thankful for on sticky notes and put them on my bathroom mirror. It was a good reminder. But my mirror got covered up pretty quickly. Then I started putting them on my bathroom walls. But I ran out of room there, too, so I put them on my toilet, the sink, the shower curtain, and the towel racks. Now I just use the downstairs bathroom.

In the *Odyssey* episode* "B-TV: Thanks" (album 31), a story was told about a rich man who gave bread to hungry children every day. When the bread was handed out one day, all the children quarreled and fought to get the biggest loaves—except for Sarah. Sarah always got the smallest loaf. But unlike the other children, she took the time to thank the man who gave it to her. The next day Sarah again got the smallest loaf, but when she got home, she noticed that the man had put three coins inside it. It was her reward for a grateful heart.

Daily Challenge

Make a list of twenty-six words, one for each letter of the alphabet, that describe the ways God is great. Do the same for things you are thankful for. Be creative with the *X*!

● ● ●

Prayer Theme Memory Verse—1 Thessalonians 5:17

Never stop praying.

---

* Want more information about this story and others on the same album? Visit *www.whitsend.org/vault*. Then browse by album and find album 31.

Devo 24

How to Pray, Part II: Confession

Today's Verse—1 John 1:9

God is faithful and fair. If we admit that we have sinned, he will forgive us our sins. He will forgive every wrong thing we have done. He will make us pure.

In 2004, Naomi Shemer finally decided to come clean. She was dying of cancer, and there was something bothering her conscience.

She was one of Israel's most famous songwriters and had written the song "Jerusalem of Gold." The beloved song had become the unofficial Israeli national anthem. But she had spent almost forty years denying the accusation that she had gotten the melody from a lullaby that had been written many decades earlier. Countless times people accused her of stealing the tune, but she consistently rejected the idea.

On her deathbed, she confessed to stealing the tune, perhaps subconsciously. She had felt bad about it many years. She said, "I consider the entire affair a regrettable work accident—so regrettable that it may be the reason for me taking ill." She actually considered that her cancer may have been caused by the guilt she felt for this secret.

The Lord's Prayer teaches us how to confess. First, it's good to admit when we do something wrong. Telling the truth about our faults keeps us humble. It also helps us remember how much we rely on God, since we're all sinners.

Second, confession helps with our feelings of guilt, because we know that God forgives sin. "Forgive me for . . ." should be a part of all of our prayers.

Third, when we confess and repent of doing wrong, it helps us know what to work on in the future. For example, if you notice that you're confessing a lot about lying,

Loquacious Learning with Eugene

Several scientific studies have linked feelings of guilt with depression. That's not terribly surprising, but guilt has been linked to physical problems as well. Sickness and disease can be caused by feelings of guilt. Confession is usually a good solution. Confessing one's sins to God and to others (especially a person you've wronged or disobeyed) will take the weight off your proverbial shoulders.

then telling the truth in the future is something you should focus on. Confession isn't all that helpful unless it's followed by repentance. So when you confess to God about lying, you also need to repent by turning away from your sin and changing your behavior with God's help.

Confession is hard, because admitting we're not perfect is hard. But there's something that's harder: keeping it all inside and being hurt by guilt. Just like Naomi Shemer did.

Daily Challenge

Think back over the past week. Is there a sin you haven't confessed yet? Have you lied? Hurt someone's feelings? Shown disrespect to an adult? Have you stolen? Disobeyed your parents? Make sure you bring these things up in your next prayer. And if you need to make anything right, do that, too.

• • •

Prayer Theme Memory Verse—1 Thessalonians 5:17

Never stop praying.

Devo 25

How to Pray, Part III: Intercession

Today's Verse—James 5:16

Pray for one another so that you might be healed. The prayer of a godly person is powerful. It makes things happen.

Rhoda was so shocked, she shut the door in the man's face. And it wasn't just any man. It was the preacher.

Oops . . . In Acts 12, Peter was put into prison for preaching about Jesus. The members of his church gathered in a house and prayed all night for him. At the same time they were praying, an earthquake hit the prison. The chains around Peter's wrists broke off. He was free!

The first place Peter went after he got out of prison was the house where his friends were praying. He knocked on the door, and a servant girl named Rhoda answered it. Rhoda was so surprised that she shut the door right in his face without even inviting him in! Instead, she ran to tell the others. They didn't believe her at first. They couldn't believe the man they were praying for was at their door. They wondered, *How did he get out of prison?*

When Rhoda finally convinced the others that Peter was there, they said, "Well, for goodness' sake, open the door!" They shouldn't have been so surprised. God answers prayer all the time.

Intercession is another part of prayer. It means praying for others. Intercession is important for many reasons. First, it helps us remember those who are struggling. Galatians 6:2 tells us that we need to "carry each other's heavy loads."

But the main reason we should pray, or intercede, for others is that prayer

Connie's Corner

When I first came to Odyssey, I wasn't a Christian. I met Whit, and he gave me a job at Whit's End. From day one he started praying for me. I didn't know it at the time, but every morning before he saw me, he prayed that I would make Jesus my Savior. I didn't stand a chance! I became a Christian, and I'm pretty sure it had a lot to do with all that praying Whit did.

works. James 5:16 says, "The prayer of a godly person is powerful. It makes things happen."

Why does prayer make things happen? *How* does it make things happen? We don't know, but many of us can tell about how prayer has worked in our own lives and in the lives of people we know. A relative is miraculously healed after doctors said there was no hope—because his family prayed for him. A family that is struggling financially suddenly receives money from a surprising source—because their church prayed for them. A college student who has rejected God all her life suddenly makes a decision for Jesus—because her parents prayed for her every day. All of these things can and do happen. And all because of intercession. What a powerful tool God has given us!

Daily Challenge

Begin a prayer notebook or a prayer calendar. Mark down people to pray for each day, and intercede for them. Then, in a few months, look back on your prayer requests and note how things worked out.

• • •

Prayer Theme Memory Verse—1 Thessalonians 5:17

Never stop praying.

Devo 26

How to Pray, Part IV: Petition

Today's Verse—Philippians 4:6

Tell God about everything. Ask and pray. Give thanks to him.

A girl with a hat shaped like a halo stepped behind the counter. "Welcome to God's throne. May I take your order?"

"Let me look at your menu," a boy said, studying the board. "All right, I'll take an A on my math test."

"Okay . . ."

"And I'd like to win my basketball game tomorrow," he added.

"Would you like to supersize that?" she asked.

"What does that mean?"

"You could be the star of the game. Score twenty points," she said.

"Ooh, yeah. Let's do that. And give me a side of courage to sit next to Lisa at lunch."

"A side of courage . . . And what do you want to drink?" she asked.

"I'll take a thirty-two-ounce cup of harsh justice for my enemies."

● ● ●

We sometimes treat prayer like this, don't we? As if God is standing behind a counter waiting for us to tell Him what we want. And then we want Him to give it to us for free.

In the *Odyssey* episode "And When You Pray . . ." (album 4), Jimmy prayed for a bike and got it. So Donna decided to pray that it would rain the next day so she could get out of gym. But all she got was laughed at, because she showed up to class in a raincoat on a sunny day. Later, at Whit's End, Whit showed the kids his new invention—a vending machine for prayers. If they pressed the buttons, they could get whatever they

Wandering with Wooton

I hate asking for stuff. Once when my car broke down,
instead of asking to borrow my neighbor's car, I
biked all the way to the store. It was fine on the way
there, but I really should have thought about the ride
home before I bought the fifteen-gallon can of olives.
With God, it's easier to ask Him for things. I know He's
listening and wants to hear what's on my heart.

wanted. But the machine didn't work, because that's not the way God works. God
wants to hear our requests, but we need to know that we won't always get what we
want. Just like a good parent, He doesn't give us everything we want.

Asking God for things for ourselves is called a petition. In the Lord's Prayer, Jesus
demonstrated how to ask for what we need ("Give us today our daily bread"), for guidance and protection ("Keep us from falling into sin when we are tempted"), and for rescue or deliverance from evil ("Save us from the evil one") (Matthew 6:11, 13). When we
petition God, we admit to Him that we can't handle problems on our own, and we want
to hand them to Him. He will help us because He loves us and wants the best for us.

Daily Challenge

When you pray this week, try hard to make petitioning God the last thing you pray
about. Make sure you honor God with praise and thanksgiving first, then confess
your sins, then ask God for His blessings on others, and finally pray for yourself. This
doesn't always have to be the order, but sometimes it helps you make sure you don't
spend your entire prayer treating God as if He were a vending machine.

• • •

Prayer Theme Memory Verse—1 Thessalonians 5:17

Never stop praying.

Devo 27

"I'm Starving!"

Today's Verse—Ezra 8:21

I told the people not to eat any food. In that way, we made ourselves low in the sight of God. We prayed that he would give us and our children a safe journey.

Have you ever made New Year's resolutions? Have you ever made one where you had to give up something? Potato chips? Television? Video games? Do you ever get to the point on January 5 where you can think *only* about potato chips?

Have you ever made a New Year's resolution that you knew you *could* keep, just so you could say that you kept one? "I'm going to give up wrestling with my brother . . . on Thursdays . . . between 4:00 and 6:00 PM . . . unless he starts it."

Fasting means giving up something for a period of time. Giving up something that's hard to give up is one of the points of fasting. It's about sacrifice. When most people think of fasting, they think of fasting from food. Jesus fasted in the wilderness for forty days after He was baptized (and before He battled with Satan). He probably did this because He knew He had a big job in front of Him. He was beginning His ministry. So He prayed and fasted to get ready for what lay ahead.

However, fasting doesn't always involve giving up food. A lot of times, it means giving up something that competes for your time with God.

In the *Odyssey* episode "Fast as I Can" (album 52), Matthew gave up computers because he thought he was spending too much time with them. Eugene gave up showing off because he thought he might be too proud of his intellect. Connie gave up primping because she thought she might be too concerned about her appearance. And Wooton gave up junk food because he knew he had bad eating habits.

Sacrificing things isn't the only point of fasting, however. The stuff you're giving

······································

Loquacious Learning with Eugene

In the early centuries of the Christian church, everyone took part in a fast around Easter time. It was for forty hours (approximately the amount of time Jesus was in the tomb). Later, the fast was expanded to forty days. On each day, Christians ate only one meal. During that time, the church would concentrate on the sacrifice Jesus made on the cross.

······································

up should be replaced by better stuff. Whenever Wooton thought about junk food, he said a little prayer for someone. This is a great way to concentrate on God during a fast.

In the Bible, people fasted when they had something important coming up. The people in the early church fasted before they appointed leaders. Acts 14:23 says, "Paul and Barnabas appointed elders for [the people] in each church. The elders had trusted in the Lord. Paul and Barnabas prayed and fasted. They placed the elders in the Lord's care."

Do you have something important coming up? A big decision that you, or someone in your family, has to make soon? Fasting might be a good way to shower that decision in prayer.

Giving up something that may be distracting you from Jesus is one way you can show your love for the One who gave His life for you on the cross!

Daily Challenge

Fast by giving up something for a day, a week, or even a month. Don't stop eating certain types of food unless you get your parents' permission. Fasting from food can be dangerous. If you do it, make sure to drink juice and take vitamins.

• • •

Prayer Theme Memory Verse—1 Thessalonians 5:17

Never stop praying.

Devo 28

Unanswered Prayers

Today's Verse—Romans 11:33

How very rich are God's wisdom and knowledge!
How he judges is more than we can understand!
The way he deals with people is more than we can know!

Garth Brooks wrote a song called "Unanswered Prayers." It's the story of a man who ran into his former high school girlfriend. The meeting brought back memories of when he wanted to marry this girl. He had prayed every night that God would give her to him. God didn't answer his prayer, but more on that later . . .

So what happens when we ask God for something and He doesn't answer? Is God asleep? Does He not care about us? The problem with the phrase "unanswered prayers" is that it's really not very accurate. God listens to every word we say. He answers every prayer. It's just that sometimes He answers no.

But why would He answer no? we wonder. *I asked for something good! Why would He do that?*

Sometimes God doesn't make sense. But here's the thing. God doesn't think like we do. For us, everything is about our lives on earth. But God thinks about things in an eternal way. James 4:14 says, "You don't even know what will happen tomorrow. What is your life? It is a mist that appears for a little while. Then it disappears."

So we don't always understand why God works the way He does. All we can do is trust that He is thinking of our best interests, and the best interests of our children, and the best interests of people we've never even met. We don't know what God knows. So we just need to trust that He loves us and is doing what is best for us.

In the Garth Brooks song, the man talked to his old girlfriend, and they had nothing to talk about. There was no love between them. He realized that this wasn't the

Whit and Wisdom

Prayer is a great gift from God. It's an honor to be able to talk to our heavenly Father at any time, for any reason. Sometimes we struggle with how to pray. Well, there are a few things you can do if you get stuck: start with "praise and thanksgiving" for God, His love, and all the things you're grateful for, then talk to Him about the things you've done wrong during the day ("confession"). Then pray for your family and friends (and even people you don't like!)—that's called "intercession." Next tell Him what's on your heart. What are you worried about? What do you need? What kind of help would you like Him to give you? That part is called "petition." Remember: God loves you more than anyone and wants to hear from you every day.

woman he was meant to marry. God had it figured out long before he had. The last lines of the song say it all:

Just because he may not answer doesn't mean he don't care . . .
Some of God's greatest gifts are unanswered prayers.

Family Challenge #4—Prayer Chart

Make a large chart for your family and put it on a bulletin board, a wall, or someplace where everyone in your family will have access to it. If something good happens to someone in your family, write it down in a "Praises" column. If there is a concern, a need, or a problem in your family, write it as a "Prayer Request." If there is an answered prayer, mark it as an "Answer." Then when your family reads through the list once a week, they can thank God for each praise or answer to prayer and pray for each request.

• • •

Prayer Theme Memory Verse—1 Thessalonians 5:17

Never stop praying.

Prayer Word Search

Find the following words about prayer in the grid.

COMMUNICATION

CONFESSION

FASTING

FORGIVENESS

INTERCESSION

LISTEN

LORDSPRAYER

PETITION

PRAISE

PRAY

REPENT

REQUESTS

THANKSGIVING

TRUST

```
P R A Y Q N O K H C D V T T R P P T
C F Y X K P F K F K G A H E S Z X R
N I E M L T I O L W C N P C P J I U
O C C R O O Y C G A Q E C M W W P S
I V V E R N N A C N N T U Y N S V T
S N N Q D F G T X T M S E R K N T S
S H T U S O B T I P F I W O W P M V
E E N E P S G H R U O L Z E K A Y F
F Q F S R S E A T W Q C Z G R P A J
N O I T A C I N U M M O C X P S T T
O P Y S Y S E K E F V H N W T A I S
C R Q U E U U S H V R J J I Z J D P
U R C R R E X G S D I N N W I W T F
Q B D T N I H I O I Z G B S P G K U
O Y N U L W Q V K B O X R D M S T H
B Y L H P E T I T I O N W O K M D U
J T G S Y H B N O D T S R R F N M L
J U Z A M D Y G L T D X Y D I O R H
```

Answers on page 239.

Bible Theme Memory Verse
Psalm 119:89

Lord, your word lasts forever. It stands firm in the heavens.

Action! Romance! War! Heroes and villains! Sparkling dialogue! Edge-of-your-seat drama! Unexpected twists and turns! An ending full of explosions, destruction, and strange creatures. Plus the good guys win! What a great movie this would make, right?

It's actually the Bible. And yes, the real-life stories in it have made some great movies. But unlike a lot of Hollywood movies, the Bible has a point. Along with all of the elements of good storytelling, the Bible is also filled with great wisdom, truth, and encouragement. Most important, the Bible is the Word of God. If we ever want to know what's on God's heart, it's in the Bible in black and white. God wanted His thoughts written down so that we can read and understand them. What a great gift.

This week we'll talk all about the Bible. It's a pretty thick book. What's in it? What does God want us to know about the world, about His Son, and about His love? What's the best way to read the Bible? How do we figure out the tough sections? All of these topics will be addressed this week as we study the amazing Word of God.

And don't be intimidated by its size. Once you start reading it, it's quite the page turner.

Prayer

Dear God,

Thank You for the Bible. Thank You for making it easy for me to understand Your heart. Help me to read Your Word, trust it, and live by its principles.

Amen.

Devo 29

What's the Big Deal About the Bible?

Today's Verse—Isaiah 40:8

The grass dries up. The flowers fall to the ground. But what our God says will stand forever.

The officer in the gray hat asked the married couple to leave the Jeep. John and Maria obeyed. They left the car and stood at the side of the road. Three other uniformed officers with guns approached the car and began to search it. Maria thought, *I'm so glad they didn't catch us on the way into the country. We might have been hanged.* John's eyes suddenly got bigger. Maria noticed. The same thought had entered both of their minds. *Oh no! The briefcase is on the front seat!*

John and Maria were Bible smugglers. In the 1960s and 1970s, owning a Bible in some Communist countries was illegal. People caught with a Bible could be arrested, tortured, or put to death. John and Maria were Americans who had come to Bulgaria to bring Bibles to people who didn't have them. On the way into the country, their Jeep had been jammed with many Bibles. John and Maria had given them all away, and they were now on their way out of the country.

Except, inside the briefcase were the names of hundreds of people inside the underground church in Bulgaria. That briefcase could lead the Bulgarian government to find these people and arrest them.

One of the officers found the briefcase and brought it to John. John simply stared at it. He didn't want to look upset or scared. That would give him away. The officer held the briefcase in front of John's eyes. John said nothing. His hands shook nervously in his pockets. The other officers called, saying they were done with the Jeep

Loquacious Learning with Eugene

The Bible is the best-selling book in human history. More than six billion copies have been sold and published—over six times as many as the second best-selling book (a book of quotations by Mao Tse-tung, if you're curious). The Bible has been translated into 2,018 languages (including the Klingon language from the *Star Trek* television show!). By comparison, the works of Shakespeare have been translated into a mere fifty languages. It isn't a stretch to say that the Bible is the most influential book ever written.

search. The officer handed John his briefcase, unopened. It was a miracle from God.

Why would John and Maria risk their lives to smuggle Bibles? Why would people inside these countries risk owning them? It is because the Bible contains truths that are so important they are worth our very lives. The Bible gives hope to hopeless people. It gives us a greater understanding of the world, and of ourselves. The Bible holds the key for finding the pathway to another life beyond this one—an eternal life in heaven. And the Bible is a love letter from God, written to a world that is desperate to know it is loved.

Daily Challenge

Find an extra Bible in your house and give it to somebody who needs one. Ask children at church, people in your neighborhood, or kids at school if they own one. The Bible will do a lot more good in the hands of someone who doesn't have one than it will in the hands of someone who has four but uses only one.

• • •

Bible Theme Memory Verse—Psalm 119:89

Lord, your word lasts forever. It stands firm in the heavens.

Devo 30

What's in the Bible?

Today's Verse—Hebrews 4:12

The word of God is living and active. It is sharper than
any sword that has two edges. It cuts deep enough to
separate soul from spirit. It can separate joints from
bones. It judges the thoughts and purposes of the heart.

In the 1960s, a group of American prisoners of war in North Vietnam had no Bible, so
they wrote a makeshift copy of their own. They called it the "Revised Prison Version."
They used the materials they had, writing the Bible on toilet paper with ink made from
cigarette ash and water. Each prisoner recited verses from memory, and those verses comprised the new Bible. Still, there were some words and lines and even large chunks missing.

The Bible's format can be easily memorized. There's an Old and a New Testament.
The Old Testament is made up of thirty-nine books. These books were all written
before Jesus was born. The New Testament is made up of twenty-seven books. These
books were all written after Jesus was born.

In the Old Testament, the first two books, Genesis and Exodus, contain great stories
about the beginning of the world. Then there's Leviticus, Numbers, and Deuteronomy,
which are filled with laws meant for people who were born before Jesus. Joshua, Judges,
Ruth, 1 and 2 Samuel, 1 and 2 Kings, 1 and 2 Chronicles, Ezra, Nehemiah, Esther, and
Job are books about fascinating folks like Joshua, Samson, Ruth, Saul, David, and Elijah.

Psalms, Proverbs, Ecclesiastes, and the Song of Solomon are books of poetry.
These books speak a lot about God, wisdom, and love. The rest of the books of the Old
Testament are books of prophecy. This means that the authors predicted certain things
about what would happen in the future. Some of these prophecies have already happened, like Jesus' birth. Some of them haven't happened yet, like the end of the world.

Wandering with Wooton

When I read I sometimes get hung up on stuff. In high school, when my English class read *A Tale of Two Cities*, I could never get past the first line. "It was the best of times, it was the worst of times." Well, which was it? But I never get hung up with the Bible. It's got exciting stories and smart advice. And the first line is way better: "In the beginning, God created the heavens and the earth ..." Tell me more!

It's not only interesting to note just how smart and godly these guys were, but also how the world hated most of them.

The New Testament starts with the four Gospels: Matthew, Mark, Luke, and John. These are books about Jesus. The book of Acts is the story of how the Christian church first began, with people like Peter, John, and Paul. The next twenty-one books are letters written by men of God, like Paul and Peter. They contain history, advice, encouragement, stern lectures, and commands of God. The last book is Revelation, which is a vision of the last days of the world that God revealed to the apostle John.

The Bible is thick, but it's worth a read; okay it's worth reading over and over and over ... It can tell us what God is like and what He wants us to be.

Daily Challenge

Look at the table of contents in your Bible and get an idea of where the books are located. If you don't recognize one of the books, turn there and see what it's about. If your Bible has introductions before each book begins, read a couple of those.

• • •

Bible Theme Memory Verse—Psalm 119:89

Lord, your word lasts forever. It stands firm in the heavens.

Devo 31

So How Should You Read the Bible?

Today's Verse—Proverbs 2:2

Let your ears listen to wisdom.
Apply your heart to understanding.

Joey decided to try something different. He decided to read a book out of order. He figured, if the words were all there, it shouldn't matter what he read first, right? So he did it. It was a book of fairy tales. He started on page 64. Then he went back to page 14. Then he decided to see how it ended, so he skipped to the last chapter. Then he turned to page 43. After fifteen minutes of reading like this, he summarized the book:

There once was a girl named Goldilocks, who ate too much porridge, so she couldn't go to the ball with her wicked stepsisters and a goose that laid poisoned apples. Then the wolf blew down her house, made out of candy. So she went to visit her grandmother, who was actually a frog in disguise. But she had to get back home, because at the stroke of midnight, her hair would grow up into the sky, and a boy named Jack would climb up and find bears in her bed. The end.

Not a very good way to read a book, is it? Yet this is often how we read the Bible. We open it up to any page, start reading, and hope we get something out of it. But when we do this, we miss out on one of the great things about the Bible: the big picture.

There are events at the beginning of the Bible that affect events at the very end. There are stories in the second half of the Bible that mean so much more when we remember stories in the first half.

Connie's Corner

Sometimes I'm a moody Bible reader. When I'm feeling sad, I read the Psalms. When I'm confused, I turn to Proverbs. And I love the book of Ruth because I'm a pushover for a good romance. But most of the time, I read the Bible in order. Lots of times I'll read a verse, and then I'll think, *That reminds me of something I read the other day* . . . And the two verses connect in interesting ways. I get so much out of the Bible when I do that.

Here are some suggestions for how to read the Bible. If you're reading the Bible for the first time, a good way to begin is to read through the Gospels—the books of Matthew, Mark, Luke, and John. But start at the beginning of each book. You won't see the big picture as clearly if you start in the middle. The beginning of the Old Testament is a good place to start too. Genesis and Exodus tell fantastic stories. If you're a slow reader, you may want to skip Leviticus, Numbers, and Deuteronomy and come back to them later. These books are about the Law, and it can be easy to get bogged down in all the details. Psalms and Proverbs are full of beautiful poetry and wisdom. Reading a bit from either of those books every day might be a good idea.

The important thing is to see the Bible as the rich book that it is. When you read it all, you'll see the wonderful story of God's love for us, from start to finish.

Daily Challenge

Pick a very short book of the Bible (for example, Philippians is only four chapters long) and read the whole thing. Write down what that book was about.

• • •

Bible Theme Memory Verse—Psalm 119:89

Lord, your word lasts forever. It stands firm in the heavens.

Devo 32

Studying the Bible

Today's Verse—2 Timothy 3:16

God has breathed life into all of Scripture. It is useful for teaching us what is true. It is useful for correcting our mistakes. It is useful for making our lives whole again. It is useful for training us to do what is right.

Here are some facts you can find in just about any encyclopedia:

- The Monroe Doctrine was enacted on December 2, 1823.
- The quadratic formula is represented by this equation:
  For $ax^2 + bx + c = 0$, the value of x is given by $x = \dfrac{b \pm \sqrt{b^2 - 4ac}}{2a}$
- One of the chief exports of Madagascar is cloves.

Do you ever wonder how you're going to use some of the information you learn? Do you think that knowing the fact about cloves will someday help you get your dream job? Unless your dream job is being an exporter in Madagascar, that's unlikely. While knowing history, math, and geography are all very important because they can help you understand the world better, sometimes it's hard to imagine a use for some of the information.

That is never true of knowing the Bible. Studying the Word of God will help you in many areas of your life, every day. The *Odyssey* episode* "The Bible Network" (album 56) takes a look at 2 Timothy 3:16: "All scripture is inspired by God, and is valuable for teaching us truth, for exposing our sin, for correcting us, and for training in righteousness" (PARAPHRASE).

The episode illustrates a different part of this verse.

In the game show "Who's the Real Sheep?" the contestant had to figure out who the

---

* To find this episode from album 56 and other episodes, visit *www.whitsend.org/vault*.

Loquacious Learning with Eugene

My area of expertise is computer technology. I have studied, at length, computer hardware, software, programming, and areas of computer technology that have yet to be conceived. I rarely learn something new about computers. But the Bible is different. Every time I study it, I come away with something I never noticed before. It's always a breath of fresh air.

false teachers were. The Bible will help you recognize the truth as well as the lies. "BSI: Bible Study Investigation" showed how the Bible exposes the sins of stealing, pride, and envy. The Bible won't let you get away with sin, because God knows how destructive it can be if it goes unchecked. The Bible can help you recognize your mistakes and correct them. "Boot Camp" has a sergeant who trained his soldiers to do what is right. The Bible can be your spiritual exercise machine. It will keep you in shape so you don't slack off and get out of good spiritual habits.

The Bible is worthy to be studied. Read it carefully. Ask a knowledgeable adult if you have any questions. Get involved in a group Bible study so you can discuss the Bible with others. You'll use this information for the rest of your life!

Daily Challenge

Memorize the Bible theme verse word for word until you have it down. Recite it in front of your parents or friends; then try reciting it backward!

• • •

Bible Theme Memory Verse—Psalm 119:89

Lord, your word lasts forever. It stands firm in the heavens.

Devo
33

What Does the Bible Mean?

Today's Verse—Psalm 119:73

You made me and formed me with your own hands. Give me understanding so that I can learn your commands.

First Thessalonians 5:17 says, "Never stop praying." What does this verse mean? Does it mean you can't sleep, talk to your friends, or think about anything else? Do you have to keep praying? What if you have to study for a history test?

There are all sorts of different ways to give meaning to the Bible. These different meanings are called *interpretations*.

In the *Odyssey* episode "The Poor Rich Guy" (album 46), Marvin and Tamika were worried about Mr. Whittaker because he had a good amount of money, and Matthew 19:24 says, "It is easier for a camel to go through the eye of a needle than for a rich man to enter the kingdom of God" (NIV). Marvin and Tamika interpreted that verse to mean that Whit wasn't going to heaven.

But Whit showed them the verses surrounding verse 24. In those verses, Jesus talked about how hard it is for a rich person to get to heaven (verse 23), but that "with God all things are possible" (verse 26, NIV). Rich people who love money more than God will have a difficult time entering heaven, but with God as their true Master, they can. Marvin and Tamika interpreted the Bible incorrectly. It's an easy trap to fall into.

Here are some tips to help you avoid getting caught in a misinterpretation. First, remember the context of the passage—when it was written, for whom it was written, and what the writer was talking about before and after the verse.

Second, your interpretation of the verse shouldn't contradict other things in the

Wandering with Wooton

I was flipping through the Bible and read this verse in Genesis: "Two of every kind of bird will come to you. Two of every kind of animal will come to you." I got scared to go outside because I thought I was gonna get overrun by a zoo! But then I kept reading and realized that God was talking to Noah. Whew! Getting the right meaning is really important!

Bible. For instance, Exodus 20:12 says, "Honor your father and mother." So you should be alert when you read Luke 14:26—"Anyone who comes to me must hate his father and mother." How can both verses be right? There must be a way to find the true meanings of *both* verses.

Third, ask someone who has studied the Bible—a pastor, your parents, a Sunday school teacher—to help you find a good Bible commentary on the Internet or at the library.

Fourth, pray for understanding. God wants you to know Him better. He will give you an answer to your questions, though sometimes you may have to wait.

Daily Challenge

In your Bible reading this week, mark down the verses you don't understand. Ask someone you trust what they mean. Write down the meanings in the margin next to the verse. Maybe you could start with 1 Thessalonians 5:17: "Never stop praying."

• • •

Bible Theme Memory Verse—Psalm 119:89

Lord, your word lasts forever. It stands firm in the heavens.

Devo 34

Bible Memorization

Today's Verse—Psalm 119:11

I have hidden your [God's] word in my heart so that I won't sin against you.

Many men like jumping across red, crazy circus goats, except Pete. Cory tried to take tomatoes to Paris. However, Joey picked precious jewels, jugs, jam, jaguars. Really!

Look carefully at the sentences above, especially the first letter of each word. It's a memory device called a *mnemonic*. Each word begins with the corresponding letter of the New Testament books in order. (**M**any **m**en **l**ike **j**umping . . . Matthew, Mark, Luke, John . . .) It's kind of a weird way to remember the first letter of the books of the New Testament, but whatever works.

Have you ever used a song to help you memorize something? How could any English speaker forget "The Alphabet Song"? A lot of people say they have poor memories, but most of the time, it's just a matter of putting their minds to it and memorizing something. How many of us know every word of that new pop song that's sweeping the nation? The same brain cells we use for memorizing songs can be used for memorizing Scripture.

In the *Odyssey* episode "Hidden in My Heart" (album 26), we heard about three reasons for memorizing Scripture. In a skit within the show called "Rescue 119," we learned that knowing Scripture will help us know when we're confronted with false teachings. In the skit "Laffie" we learned that we need to know Scripture in case we're confronted with a moral dilemma, or if we need to tell someone else about Jesus. In the skit "Star Trip" we learned that knowing Scripture keeps us from falling into temptation, because we'll recognize when we're in the presence of it.

Connie's Corner

When I was in high school, I had to memorize all the kings of England. Augh! It was so hard because I didn't know the difference between Henry VIII and John CXVIII (or whoever he was). But Philippians 4:13–"I can do everything by the power of Christ. He gives me strength"–now that's something I can memorize, because it means something important! Oh, I'm sorry. Philippians IV:XIII. *Augh!*

Here are some tips for memorizing Scripture verses:

- The most important tip is to attach meaning to the words you're memorizing. Memorizing words is difficult, but memorizing ideas is easier.
- Write the entire verse on a white board and say it aloud numerous times, erasing one word every time.
- Say the verse through the day, over and over. Memorizing for five minutes from 12:00 to 12:05 isn't as effective as memorizing a verse for one minute at noon, again at 1:00, again at 1:45, and so on.

However you do it, hiding God's Word in your heart is one of the best ways to build a strong relationship with God.

Daily Challenge

With your parents' permission, visit *www.godtube.com* and search for Bible songs. There are plenty of clips that will help you memorize the books of the Bible. Pick one and learn at least the first ten books of the New Testament.

● ● ●

Bible Theme Memory Verse—Psalm 119:89

Lord, your word lasts forever. It stands firm in the heavens.

Devo 35

"So What's It to Me?"

Today's Verse—Ephesians 6:17

And take the sword of the Holy Spirit. The sword is God's word.

King Darius put Daniel in charge of the whole kingdom, and the royal rulers weren't happy about it. The rulers, who knew that Daniel prayed to God every day, told Darius to make it a law that if someone was caught praying to anyone other than Darius himself, that person would be put to death. But praying every day was important to Daniel, so he kept right on praying.

The king found out and reluctantly gave the order to throw Daniel into a den of lions. The royal rulers were happy that Daniel would soon be dead. But the next morning when the den was opened, Daniel was alive and safe. God had protected him from the lions' jaws. King Darius was glad that God had spared Daniel's life, and he threw the royal rulers into the lions' den instead. (You can read the full story in Daniel 6.)

This is an exciting story, and most of us have heard it. But is that all it is? Isn't there something more we can learn from it? And more important, is there something helpful we can learn from it that we can use in our own lives?

Look at the story again and think about the lessons it teaches. (1) *Avoid jealousy.* The royal rulers were envious of Daniel's position, and they ended up paying for it with their lives. Now apply that to your life. Is there any jealousy in your heart? Are you envious of your brother's athletic ability? Your friend's intelligence? (2) *Prayer is powerful.* Daniel wouldn't stop praying to God, even though he knew it could mean the end of his life. How important is prayer to you? (3) *God gives courage.* Daniel had the courage to stand up for what he believed in. Is there a situation you're dealing with right now that requires courage? (4) *God grants protection.* God kept Daniel alive because God loved him. Is there anything you're afraid of?

Whit and Wisdom

Connie convinced me to go to a movie with her the other day. It was a comedy and we joined some other people from the church. I read about the movie first and thought it was harmless, so I went. About halfway through, right after the third time the main character had told a really unfunny joke, I decided I'd seen enough. I slipped out into the lobby, pulled out my pocket New Testament, and began reading. It was so much more interesting than the movie, and a better use of my time!

Sometimes I think about all the time we spend doing things that don't really matter. We do one thing or another, wasting our time away, when we have the very heart and words of God at our fingertips. God longs for us to know Him better. Reading the Bible is the best way I know to do that.

Perhaps you should trust that God will protect you, just as He protected Daniel.

So now you know what's in the Bible, you know the importance of the Bible, and you've even memorized some of it. But none of that will mean anything if you don't apply the lessons of the Bible. The Bible has a lot to say to us. Read it and find out what God has to say to you.

Family Challenge #5—Bible Trivia

Have a Bible trivia contest. One of your parents could be the host. You can play it like a real game show. Categories could be Bible Stories, Bible Verses, or Books of the Bible. Include prizes for the winners. You should have fun with it, but it could also be a great time of learning for the whole family.

• • •

Bible Theme Memory Verse—Psalm 119:89

Lord, your word lasts forever. It stands firm in the heavens.

The Bible Code

Find the rest of the letters in the Bible verse on the next page, which was taken from the book of Psalms. The grid is your code box. Figure out the rest of the letters of the code, and you'll be able to finish the verse. Hint: You have to guess at the letters from the verse and figure the code out by trial and error. Can you guess which word in the verse is THE? What number is E?

Puzzle #5

A	B	C	D	E	F	G	H	I	J	K	L	M
13					11		26	8				

N	O	P	Q	R	S	T	U	V	W	X	Y	Z
				1					23			

		R		,			R		W		R			A			
7	24	1	18		4	24	16	1		23	24	1	18		7	13	21	10	21

F		R				R	.		I				A		
11	24	1	20	6	20	1		8	10		21	10	13	25	18	21

F	I	R			I			H			H		A				
11	8	1	5		8	25		10	26	20		26	20	13	6	20	25	21

Answers on page 240.

91

Exercising Faith Theme Memory Verse

Hebrews 11:1

Faith is being sure of what we hope for. It is being certain of what we do not see.

Daredevil Charles Blondin was either very brave or very crazy. On June 30, 1859, he stretched a tightrope across Niagara Falls, about 200 feet above the gorge. Facing certain death if he fell, he walked across it. On later occasions, Blondin went back to perform the feat again—once with a sack over his head, once while carrying another man on his back, and one more time when he brought a stove and cooking utensils with him. When he got to the middle of the wire, he sat down and fried an omelet!

Blondin had to have a lot of faith in a lot of things to risk his life like that. He had to have faith in the strength of the wire. He had to have faith in his teammates on the other side of the river—that they had done a good job anchoring the wire. He had to have faith in his own abilities. He had to have faith that he wouldn't lose his balance and fall to his death.

Sometimes putting faith in God seems just as hard. No one can see God. And yet so many have staked their lives on Him.

This week, we're going to talk about faith in God. What is it? Why should we have it? And once we have it, what kinds of actions should faith inspire? Believing in God is similar to walking on a high wire over Niagara Falls. (And while we want you to test your faith in God, we don't want you to try tightrope walking unless you belong to the circus!) There is risk involved in both activities. But once we make it to the other side of the faith chasm, we will see that having faith in God is completely worth it.

Prayer

Dear God,

Thank You for giving me so much reason to have faith in You. Help me to believe in Your power, Your control over my life, and Your love for me.

Amen.

Devo 36

What Is Faith?

Today's Verse—2 Chronicles 20:20

Have faith in the Lord your God. He'll take good care of you.

We show our faith in everyday life even when we don't realize we're doing it. We get into our cars to drive across town, having faith that when we step on the brake pedal, the car will stop. If we didn't have that kind of faith in our brakes, we would drive a lot more slowly. We exercise faith when we get on elevators. Are we sure that a cable will hold a lift full of people? I guess we are. We have faith that the food we just ordered at a restaurant won't make us sick. Are we certain that the farmers who picked this food can tell the difference between a safe mushroom and a poisonous one? We don't know any of these things for sure. We just have faith.

Hebrews 11:1 says," Faith is being sure of what we hope for. It is being certain of what we do not see." But faith is also strengthened by evidence. We believe in our car brakes because they've worked every other time we've used them. This is also true of elevators. And we rarely experience food poisoning at a restaurant, so we trust that the food is safe.

The same is true of our faith in God. God has worked things out for us in the past, and so we can have complete faith in Him that He will look out for our best interests in the future. Before Noah built his ark, the Bible says that "the Lord was pleased with Noah" (Genesis 6:8). Noah was already a man of God. He had already seen evidence of God working in his life. But, boy, did Noah have to have a lot of faith to do what he did!

In the *Odyssey* episode* "By Faith, Noah" (album 4), Whit told a funny version of the story of Noah. When God asked Noah to build a huge boat, Noah probably

---

* To find more Adventures in Odyssey Bible stories, visit *www.whitsend.org/vault*. To date, there are at least thirty shows taken directly from the Bible.

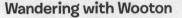

Wandering with Wooton

Before I became a Christian, I had a Magic Eight Ball. I asked the ball questions, and it would give me answers. I'd ask, "Will I be famous one day?" and it would say, "Doubtful"; then I'd be depressed for a week. It was a pretty silly thing to put my faith in. Now I ask God my important questions. He doesn't always give me an answer right away, but at least He's a lot more accurate than that ball.

thought the whole idea was nuts. But he had faith in God, so he built the ark. In Whit's story, Noah had to deal with his neighbors who mocked him, city health inspectors, the president of the Ark Builders Union, and others. But Noah kept building. For 120 years he hammered, sawed, sanded, and buffed. Noah's faith paid off for him because he and his family ended up being the only people on the planet to survive a flood.

Do you believe that God will take care of you? That God is always looking out for you? That God loves you? The evidence is all around you, but when it comes right down to it, you simply have to have faith.

Daily Challenge

In your Bible reading this week, make note of all the people who had to have faith. How did they show their faith? What did they risk by having faith? How were they rewarded by having faith?

• • •

Exercising Faith Theme Memory Verse—Hebrews 11:1

Faith is being sure of what we hope for. It is being certain of what we do not see.

Devo 37

The Power of Faith

Today's Verse—Mark 5:34

[Jesus] said to her, "Dear woman, your faith has healed you. Go in peace. You are free from your suffering."

The woman falls to her knees. The water splashes up out of the bucket and drenches her dress. She buries her head in her hands and weeps aloud. For twelve years it has hurt, but never been like this.

A man hears her wailing. He bends to help her up. The woman raises her hand to tell him no. She just wants to sit on the ground for a while. The man says kindly, "I have heard of a man who heals."

The woman shakes her head. "The doctors don't know why I'm bleeding inside. They can't help."

The man says, "This one isn't a doctor. He heals by the power of God. His name is Jesus."

The woman looks up at him. She believes in God. She believes God can heal her. She must not pass up this opportunity. She leaves the bucket on the ground and goes. She must find Jesus. It is a long, painful journey for her, but she finds Him. People crowd around Him so thickly it is hard to even catch a glimpse. But she moves closer. Suddenly, pain stabs her. She doubles over. She can barely move. But Jesus is close. So close. She threads her way through the crowd, still bent over.

If I just touch the hem of His garment, then I will be healed.

With one last desperate effort, she lunges. Her fingertips lightly brush the bottom of His robe. Jesus stops suddenly. The crowd grows quiet.

He says, "Who touched me?" He turns around and sees the woman on her knees. She looks back at Him. The power of God courses through her body. Her bleeding

Connie's Corner

I totally believe that faith in God heals us. And not just our bodies. God can heal us from any kind of problem. He can even heal us through the faith of other people, not just through our own faith! My mother got really sick once, and the whole church prayed for her. The doctors were surprised at how quickly she recovered. And this was before my mom had become a Christian. Faith is really powerful.

stops. She is healed. Suddenly she is afraid. *Is He angry with me?* she wonders. She nervously looks into His eyes. "I touched you," she says simply.

Jesus says, "Dear woman, your faith has healed you" (Mark 5:25–34).

• • •

How about you? Like this woman, do you turn to God when you're scared or sick or hurting? Sometimes we panic and rush around doing everything *except* pray and ask God for help. But God is the true Healer, and He loves it when we come to Him in faith.

Daily Challenge

Get in the habit of praying for sick or hurting people. Every day, try to remember one or two people who are struggling with their health or another problem.

• • •

Exercising Faith Theme Memory Verse—Hebrews 11:1

Faith is being sure of what we hope for. It is being certain of what we do not see.

"Dude, Where's My Faith?"

Today's Verse—1 Thessalonians 5:16–18

Always be joyful. Never stop praying.
Give thanks no matter what happens.

You waited for it for weeks. Every time you saw it in the store, you dropped not-so-subtle hints to your mom. You tore out ads for it and put one on the refrigerator . . . and a few in your dad's car . . . and enough on the mirror to wallpaper the bathroom.

Then, on your birthday, you tore through the wrapping paper and saw it—the UltraMegaWhangdoodler 5000. You shouted so loud that the neighbors complained . . . the ones four houses down. For the next few weeks, you played with the Whangdoodler constantly. Your friends had to wear gloves to even touch it.

Then, as the weeks passed, the Whangdoodler wasn't as exciting, and you moved on to other things. Eventually, it got shoved under the bed with a few old magazines, half a bag of stale pretzels, and your gum wrapper collection.

Even the coolest toys and gadgets can get boring pretty quickly. Sometimes our faith can be like that too. We have great experiences, like at a church camp, and then we want to change the world for Jesus. But at other times, we feel as if our relationship with God just isn't going anywhere. Going to church is boring, and reading the Bible doesn't seem very important.

This happened in the Bible to a church in Ephesus. God told the people in that church, "But here is something I hold against you. You don't have as much love as you had at first" (Revelation 2:4). But God gave them the cure for lost love in the next verse: "Turn away from your sins. Do the things you did at first" (verse 5).

Wandering with Wooton

I love being a mailman. But sometimes I don't feel like being one. Especially when it's the day for those thick catalogs to be delivered. *Augh!* But just because I don't like those catalogs doesn't mean I stop delivering them. The same is true of being a Christian. Some days it's harder to get excited about my faith. But I still know it's there cause I had it yesterday and the day before. Don't get me started about those really thick Bibles, though!

In the *Odyssey* episode "Harlow Doyle, Private Eye" (album 14), Jessie asked the detective to find her lost faith. As it turned out, she hadn't really lost her faith at all. She had simply failed to do the things that strengthened her faith. She had stopped attending church, and she read silly teen magazines instead of the Bible. Her faith was still there. She just needed to give it a boost.

What's the key to a strong faith? Keep praying, keep reading your Bible, and keep worshipping, even when you don't feel inspired to do it. And don't worry if you don't feel strong in your faith all the time. Faith isn't something that can be measured by feelings. It's something you commit to, even if the feelings come and go.

Daily Challenge

The next time something bad happens, immediately go to the Lord in prayer. Have faith that He is listening, even when things around you don't feel like they're going right.

• • •

Exercising Faith Theme Memory Verse—Hebrews 11:1

Faith is being sure of what we hope for. It is being certain of what we do not see.

Devo 39

Faith and Science

° °

Today's Verse—Psalm 139:14

How you made me is amazing and wonderful. I praise you for that. What you have done is wonderful. I know that very well.

° °

Our bodies are totally amazing! Here are some cool findings from the *Reader's Digest Book of Facts* and other sources . . .

- It's possible for the human nose to recognize fifty thousand different scents.
- If all the blood vessels in your body were strung end to end, they would stretch around the world two and a half times.
- Bones are four times stronger than concrete.
- Nerve impulses from your brain to your arms and legs travel at 170 miles per hour.

Can you believe that some people actually think that the human body has no Creator? That it just "happened"? That the human body somehow formed on its own from random cells moving around? How could anyone look at how incredible the human body is and not be amazed by the One who obviously created it?

Others believe that the natural world happened all by itself. That there are scientific explanations for everything, and that there is no room for God in the equation.

Scientist and famous atheist Richard Dawkins once said, "Faith is the great cop-out, the great excuse to evade the need to think and evaluate evidence." That guy needs to stop talking, because he doesn't know what he's talking about.

Faith isn't the absence of thought, and it's not a cop-out! It is completely logical and reasonable to look at the world around you and believe that it had a Creator—that's faith.

Just because you believe in God doesn't mean you have to stop thinking or

Loquacious Learning with Eugene

Before I became a Christian, I admit to having difficulty combining the ideas of science and faith. Now I look back and I can't even see how I could look at things any differently. It is estimated that there are one hundred thousand million stars in our universe. How can you deny the existence of a God big enough to create them all?

believing in science! There is a lot of scientific evidence that supports the existence of God.

Perhaps the most famous scientist of all time, Albert Einstein, said, "I want to know how God created this world, I am not interested in this or that phenomenon, in the spectrum of this or that element. I want to know his thoughts, the rest are details." If only all scientists were as smart as Einstein!

When you think about it, faith is kind of easy at times. It's easy to look at the world and believe in the magnificent God who created all of it. The more you look at the world, the more you see God's fingerprints all over the place.

Daily Challenge

Go on the Internet (with your parents' permission) or visit the library to find information about the human body. Write down ten amazing facts and present them to your family. Thank God for being such an incredible Inventor.

• • •

Exercising Faith Theme Memory Verse—Hebrews 11:1

Faith is being sure of what we hope for. It is being certain of what we do not see.

Devo 40

Faith Through the Tough Stuff

Today's Verse—Psalm 30:5

Sobbing can remain through the night.
But joy comes in the morning.

Horatio Spafford had a happy life. He was married with five children, and he owned his own business in Chicago in the 1860s. He was also a man of faith. And he would need every ounce of that faith to get through what was about to happen.

First his four-year-old son died of scarlet fever. Later the Great Chicago Fire of 1871 destroyed everything in its path. Spafford lost his business and almost everything he owned. Then he sent his wife and four daughters on a ship to England. He planned to meet them there later. The ship sank in a storm. Only his wife survived.

After the shipwreck, Spafford sailed to England to meet his wife. As Spafford's ship crossed the Atlantic Ocean, the captain pointed out to Spafford where the ship that had carried his family had gone down. It was at this spot where Spafford wrote a hymn of praise to God.

What would lead a man to write a hymn of praise to God when such terrible things had happened to him? It was this: Spafford had faith that God was still in control. He believed with all his heart that God still loved him and wanted what was best for him. Spafford knew that his sorrow would end, especially on that day when he would go to heaven to spend eternity with his children.

Is there anything you're going through right now that is making you doubt that God loves you? Bad things happen sometimes, and it's difficult to understand what

Connie's Corner

The week my grandmother died was one of the worst weeks of my life. I loved her, and it was really hard to say good-bye. She used to sing hymns to me when I was a little girl. Now I imagine her singing those hymns in heaven, with Jesus sitting right next to her. She must be so happy. I still miss her, but knowing she's having such a good time makes it a little better.

God is doing. Talk to someone about it if you're hurting. Pray for understanding and strength to get through the tragedy. And most important, pray for the faith of Horatio Spafford, who wrote the inspired hymn "It Is Well with My Soul":

When peace, like a river, attendeth my way,
When sorrows like sea billows roll—
Whatever my lot, Thou hast taught me to say,
It is well, it is well with my soul.

Daily Challenge

Listen to the *Odyssey* episode "It Is Well" (album 16) and hear the Horatio Spafford story for yourself. Then ask God to help you have the same faith Horatio had.

• • •

Exercising Faith Theme Memory Verse—Hebrews 11:1

Faith is being sure of what we hope for. It is being certain of what we do not see.

Devo 41

The Silent Singer

Today's Verse—James 2:14

> My brothers and sisters, what good is it if
> people claim they have faith but don't act like it?

"Hi, I'm Joel. Nice to meet you, Sarah. What do you do?" Joel extended his hand to shake hers.

"I'm a singer," Sarah said.

"Oh, really. Where do you sing?"

"Nowhere."

"You don't sing?"

"Never," Sarah said.

"Not even in the shower?" Joel asked.

"Nope."

"You're a singer who doesn't sing?"

"That's right."

"In that case," Joel said, "I'm a brain surgeon who's never done brain surgery."

A person of faith who doesn't show his or her faith is like a singer who doesn't sing. James 2:15–17 says, "Suppose a brother or sister has no clothes or food. Suppose one of you says to them, 'Go. I hope everything turns out fine for you. Keep warm. Eat well.' And you do nothing about what they really need. Then what good have you done? It is the same with faith. If it doesn't cause us to do something, it's dead."

As Christians, we're to show that we have faith in God by doing the things God asks us to do. God wants us to read our Bibles, pray, worship Him, be servants to others, love our neighbors, be involved in a church, give offerings, share our faith with others, and be people of integrity so that non-believers will see our dedication to

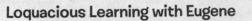

Loquacious Learning with Eugene

Astronauts, after just a few days in space, have been known to develop a condition that causes the muscles to waste away. The close confines of a spacecraft make it difficult to exercise, and the lack of gravity means there is no natural resistance to keep the muscles strong and healthy. Our faith needs to have resistance as well. It needs to be challenged for us to stay spiritually healthy.

God. We have to do these things or our faith will wither. Exercising our faith is the only way to keep it strong.

Real faith is more than words. We need to show how much we love God by obeying Him.

Daily Challenge

Create a daily Faith Workout Routine. Make sure you're doing the things every day that God requires of you to build up your spiritual muscles—pray, read the Bible, and be a servant to others.

• • •

Exercising Faith Theme Memory Verse—Hebrews 11:1

Faith is being sure of what we hope for. It is being certain of what we do not see.

Devo
42

That Last Step Is a Doozy!

Today's Verse—Proverbs 16:3

Commit to the Lord everything you do. Then your plans will succeed.

Two-year-old Michael shuffled his feet toward the edge of the pool. He looked down at the water. Then he looked at his dad standing in the pool. His dad's arms were opened wide.

"Come on, Michael. Jump! I'll catch you, I promise!"

Michael inched a little closer to the side of the pool. He stopped looking at the water and looked into his father's eyes. With every ounce of courage he could muster, he closed his eyes . . . and jumped.

That was a big moment for Michael, wasn't it? But you know what? As big a moment as it was for Michael, it was an even bigger one for Michael's father. *Michael trusts me*, he probably thought. *My son knows I will be there.*

God loves it when we take leaps of faith into His arms as well. God has done so much to prove Himself to us, and when we trust Him enough to take a risk, He's pleased.

So what kinds of leaps can you take to show your faith in God? Is there a lonely kid at your school or in your neighborhood that you can befriend? It takes a leap of faith to reach out to someone you don't know.

Your parents sometimes have to make leaps of faith with their jobs. You might have to move away from your home because your parents believe that God is calling your family somewhere else. Trusting your parents' judgment instead of throwing a fit about moving is a leap of faith.

It's hard, isn't it? But if you decide to leap, God will be there to catch you!

Whit and Wisdom

Y'know, considering all the things God has done for us, you think it'd be easy to have faith in Him. But sometimes we have a hard time seeing or remembering what God has done. And even though we try not to have doubts, they show up anyway.

Why? Well, one reason is that we can't actually see God. Or can we?

The marvelous thing about God is that, even though we can't see Him, we can see evidence of Him. The beauty He has created. The wonders of His creation. We can see how His love fills people around us. We can pick up His Word–the Bible–and read the testimonies of His great work throughout history.

That's why we need to give our faith a daily workout. Look around you. Stop for a moment and ask God to remind you that He's around. That's how we keep faith alive. And as our faith grows, so will our experience of God.

Family Challenge #6—Finding Faith History

As a family, compile stories of faith. Call your grandparents and pastor and see if they have witnessed, or lived out, a strong faith during difficult times. Search the Internet and the library about people of faith like John Bunyan, William Wilberforce, or Fanny Crosby. When you've finished gathering stories, share them with your family. Then pray to be a family of strong faith.

• • •

Exercising Faith Theme Memory Verse—Hebrews 11:1

Faith is being sure of what we hope for. It is being certain of what we do not see.

Faith Find

Match the clue with the correct scrambled word.

1. Being certain of what we do not see.
2. Famous scientist who believed in God.
3. James 2:17 says that faith without works is this.
4. These people often get a condition where muscle wastes away.
5. Last name of the author of the hymn "It Is Well with My Soul."
6. Bones are four times stronger than this.
7. The woman who had been bleeding for twelve years touched the hem of Jesus' ____.
8. First Thessalonians 5:17 says to never stop ____.
9. ___ of faith.
10. There are 1,000,000,000,000,000,000,000 of these in our universe.

Puzzle #6

A. TNGMEAR

B. IHFTA

C. NNIESETI

D. RAPGINY

E. TCEONREC

F. RTSAS

G. EDAD

H. FOSAPFDR

I. ALEP

J. STRAONSTUA

Answers on page 241.

----- THEME SEVEN -----

Forgiveness

Forgiveness Theme Memory Verse
Ephesians 4:32

Be kind and tender to one another. Forgive each other, just as God forgave you because of what Christ has done.

ODYSSEY

Do you know what Corrie ten Boom, Pope John Paul II, Elisabeth Elliot, and Kim Phuc have in common?

I'll give you a hint: All these famous people had something bad happen to them. Need more help? Something bad happened to each of them, and that bad something wasn't an accident—it was done on purpose.

Corrie ten Boom was captured by the Nazis and sent to a concentration camp during World War II. Her father and sister both died as a result of the Nazis' brutality.

In 1981 Pope John Paul II was shot four times by a would-be assassin named Mehmet Ali Agca.

Elisabeth Elliot's husband, Jim, was a missionary to Ecuador in the 1950s and was murdered by a group of Auca Indians.

Kim Phuc lived in Vietnam. In 1972 she was a young girl, and her village was destroyed by napalm bombs. The chemicals hurt her so badly that she had to have seventeen surgeries and still lives in pain today.

But those bad things weren't the end of these people's stories. All of these bad situations ended in forgiveness.

Corrie ten Boom forgave a Nazi prison guard (who later became a Christian). Pope John Paul II forgave Mehmet Ali Agca, going to the shooter's prison cell to tell him in person. Elisabeth Elliot went to Ecuador and served as a missionary to the very people who murdered her husband. And Kim Phuc publicly forgave the people who bombed her village.

In this theme we'll talk about the greatest story of forgiveness of all—when Jesus Christ died on the cross. That's not the end of the story. We'll look at how His story can change your life for the better.

Prayer

Dear God,

Whenever someone hurts me, show me how to forgive the person. Then help me live my life in a way that is worthy of Your example. Thank You for Your ever-present gift of forgiveness.

Amen.

Devo
43

The Public Defender

Today's Verse—Psalm 103:10

[God] doesn't punish us for our sins as much
as we should be punished. He doesn't pay us
back in keeping with the evil things we've done.

Imagine being in a courtroom. The Judge is in front of you. Your mother is behind you, and you've broken her heart. She's sobbing. What have you done?

You've cheated on a math test, and this Judge has a no-tolerance policy. You will flunk the school year and be condemned to an eternity without hope or fun of any kind. You sigh.

You're not the first to stand in this courtroom. Adam and Eve were. They carved their initials on the table in front of you. Maybe you should do that too, but there isn't much space. Billions of initials are there. Your heart breaks for the pain you are causing your family. Your sister, who is sitting next to your mother, starts crying too.

Only someone perfect would be able to satisfy this Judge. You glance sideways at your public defender. He's the Judge's Son, He's perfect, and He isn't a descendant of Adam and Eve. You sigh again. He would never understand what it's like to be a cheater, what it's like to be on this side of the Judge's bench.

Still, He's your only hope, so you turn to Him and say, "Jesus, I'm guilty. You're the only One who can help me." He gives you a quick nod and a half smile.

Before the Judge can sentence you, or even finish reading your case, Jesus steps forward and says, "My client is guilty. I'll take the blame."

With that, you're forgiven. The Judge says to you, "You're free to go." That's when you notice all the scars on Jesus' body and realize that He's already died in your place. He was just waiting for you to acknowledge that He was the only way

Connie's Corner

Sometimes I feel as if people are stepping on me. But when I forgive them, it's as if I release what they did so their meanness can't affect me anymore. I trade something ugly for something beautiful. That's what God wants me to do. He wants me to do what's right, no matter how others act. Sometimes it means I have to sacrifice my pride so I can forgive. When I do that, though, my life goes so much better.

out of your sins. Now your sins—all of them   have been forgiven as if you were a fully innocent person.

Daily Challenge

On a piece of paper, write down five reasons that you should NOT forgive someone. Then tear up the list. If Jesus has forgiven your sins, you have no reason to withhold forgiveness from someone else.

• • •

Forgiveness Theme Memory Verse—Ephesians 4:32

Be kind and tender to one another. Forgive each other, just as God forgave you because of what Christ has done.

Devo 44

Live Fully

Today's Verse—Luke 6:37

If you do not judge others, then you will not be judged. If you do not find others guilty, then you will not be found guilty. Forgive, and you will be forgiven.

Joseph had every right to get even with his brothers. They had thrown him into a well and sold him into slavery. Nice guys. But then his life went from bad to worse. He was wrongfully accused of a crime, thrown into an Egyptian prison, and left to die.

After many years, God caused Pharaoh to put Joseph in charge of all the food in his kingdom. When Joseph's brothers came to Egypt to buy food for their starving families, they didn't recognize him. Joseph now had the power to get even with them. But he didn't.

"You are spies," Joseph said accusingly.

They assured him they weren't. Eventually Joseph gave them food and allowed them to return home, but he kept one brother in prison until they came back to Egypt. He needed to know if they'd changed. When they returned, they brought their youngest brother, Benjamin, to prove they weren't spies. But Joseph still didn't know whether they were sorry for what they'd done to him. So the second time they prepared to leave Egypt, he made it look like Benjamin had stolen one of his expensive cups.

"As punishment," Joseph said, "Benjamin will stay in Egypt."

"Take me instead," said one of his brothers. "Our father will die if Benjamin doesn't return."

That's when Joseph knew his brothers had changed. "I am Joseph, your brother," he told them.

Loquacious Learning with Eugene

An atom is so small that you can't see it without an electron microscope. And every atom has a nucleus at its center. The nucleus is usually a stable part of the atom. Unstable nuclei send out particles called radiation. If the nucleus of an atom is split or if two small atoms are forced together, heat and radiation are released. Not forgiving others can be compared to an unstable nucleus. It is a miniscule thing, but under the proper conditions, it can lead to an enormous explosion.

At first his brothers were scared. They knew he had the power to get even with them.

But Joseph said, "What you meant for evil, God used for good."

Joseph had realized that God's purpose for his life didn't depend on his brothers' actions. He had let go of the mean things that his brothers had done to him so he could fully live the life God wanted for him. To let go, Joseph chose to forgive his brothers. (For the whole story, see Genesis chapters 37, 39–45.)

Daily Challenge

Be especially nice to your siblings this week and try to do what is right by them. If you're an only child, choose a friend to treat especially well, the way Joseph treated others.

• • •

Forgiveness Theme Memory Verse—Ephesians 4:32

Be kind and tender to one another. Forgive each other, just as God forgave you because of what Christ has done.

Devo 45

Socks and Showers

Today's Verse—Luke 17:3

If your brother sins, tell him he is wrong.
Then if he turns away from his sins, forgive him.

Sam liked soccer, but he hated showers and scowled at soap. Soap was slippery, and shampoo stung his eyes. As seasons passed, Sam shamefully decided he was done suffering through showers. So he washed his face, strands of his hair, and his hands. Then he slipped into a new pair of socks. To others, he seemed clean.

This worked for some time. Then one day his soiled toes became slimy, and his socks stuck to his feet. Sam washed as usual, but this time he didn't slip off his old socks. Instead, he slipped clean socks over his soiled ones.

The next day, the slime oozed through his second pair of socks. The second pair now stuck to Sam's first set of socks, which stuck to his toes. So Sam slid another clean pair over the second pair. But by the seventh day of doing this, Sam struggled to shove his socked feet into his shoes. And once he did get his feet into his shoes, he let out a shriek of pain.

Sam's parents saw what Sam was doing, so they cut off his slimy socks with scissors and sent him to the shower.

• • •

Surprisingly, Sam's seven socks and his shower struggles show something about forgiveness. When you fail to forgive someone, it's as if you have slimy feet that you are covering with clean socks. Not forgiving soils your life and will eventually keep you from being cleansed from the stench of slime known as bitterness and anger.

In the *Odyssey* episode "Forgive Us as We Forgive" (album 17), Eric refused to

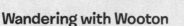

Wandering with Wooton

Imagine that Captain Absolutely is caught in the middle of a very slimy situation. He's battling the Unforgiveness Monster that's made of nothing but snails, slugs, sludge, and stinky stuff. His only way out is to cut the monster down to size. It's the same way for us when we don't forgive someone—we're caught in a slimy mess of slithering stuff. The only way out is to be willing to forgive. The Captain's motto should be: Forgiveness—It takes the slime out of life!

forgive his father. His unwillingness soon hurt their relationship and Eric's relationships with others in his family.

Luke 17:3 says, "If your brother sins, tell him he is wrong. Then if he turns away from his sins, forgive him." Only forgiveness can release you from bitterness and anger.

Daily Challenge

Think of one thing you've done that you would like a do-over for—something you've done that's hurt someone. Write it down on a sheet of paper and put it in a safe place. Whenever you don't want to forgive someone, read the paper. Remember that you have the power to give someone else a do-over by forgiving him or her.

• • •

Forgiveness Theme Memory Verse—Ephesians 4:32

Be kind and tender to one another. Forgive each other,
just as God forgave you because of what Christ has done.

Devo 46

A Historical Apology

Today's Verse—Matthew 6:12

Forgive us our sins, just as we also have
forgiven those who sin against us.

John Adams and Thomas Jefferson are a part of American history. They both declared America's independence, and they both became US presidents. They were also good friends.

At first they believed many of the same things and helped each other. They even spent time in France together. They wanted the French government to help the American colonies fight their war for independence.

Over time these two men found they also had differences. For a while they figured out ways to have opposite opinions and be friends. But then they each went too far with their differences, and their friendship ended.

One day years later, Jefferson heard that Adams had complimented him. Jefferson wrote Adams a letter, and Adams wrote back. These two men chose to forgive each other and become friends again. They remained friends for the rest of their lives.

When you're close to someone, it doesn't mean you like all the same things or always want to do the same stuff. It also doesn't mean that you won't mess up or treat each other poorly. But it does mean you'll have the opportunity to forgive each other.

In the *Odyssey* episode* "Call Me If You Care" (album 43), Connie learned how easy it is to become estranged from someone in your family that you love. After forgiving her father, Connie tried to find a way to reconnect with him.

---

* Want to listen to more episodes written by Nathan Hoobler, as this one was? Visit *www.whitsend. org/vault* and look for the area that says "Browse by Production Crew."

Connie's Corner

I try to treat people well, but sometimes I offend somebody even when I don't mean to. In those cases, forgiveness is like a secret weapon that can set things right. When I say I'm sorry and ask for forgiveness, I let go of my emotions and can see the situation in a new way. This helps my friend and me enjoy each other's company once again.

Like Connie, you may realize that your family and friends aren't the same as you. And they don't always act as you expect them to. The solution: You can allow them to be the people they are and forgive them when they disappoint you. Because Jefferson and Adams forgave each other, they were able to enjoy a close friendship for many, many years. In their later years, they wrote letters to each other. Surprisingly they died on the same day.

Daily Challenge

Write down three ways you might accidentally hurt a friend. Remember these things the next time someone upsets you. It may help you forgive this person.

• • •

Forgiveness Theme Memory Verse—Ephesians 4:32

Be kind and tender to one another. Forgive each other,
just as God forgave you because of what Christ has done.

Devo 47

Asking for Forgiveness

Today's Verse—Romans 12:18

If possible, live in peace with everyone.
Do that as much as you can.

A child wrote this apology for misbehaving:

I'm sorry for the spilled milk,
I'm sorry for the bread,
I'm sorry that I threw it
At Tommy Tucker's head.
I'm sorry for my actions
And shouting this at you;
It's woken up the baby
Before the morning dew.
I'm sorry to have woke you,
I'm sorry that I fought;
But mostly I am sorry
Because I have been caught.

Is the child in this poem truly sorry? No, he isn't. He's misbehaving even as he's apologizing. That isn't how a true apology works.

In the *Odyssey* episode "The Homecoming" (album 10), Richard Maxwell wanted to tell five people in Odyssey that he was sorry for his wrong actions. And, unlike the child in the poem, Richard meant it. Richard chose to apologize and ask for forgiveness. Four characters agreed to forgive him. But the final person, Tom Riley, refused.

THEME SEVEN

Forgiveness

Loquacious Learning with Eugene

Considering our legal theme, I believe that it would be helpful to point out that the path to forgiveness requires the first party, hereafter known as the wrongdoer, to present himself (or herself, if the case may be) before a second party, hereafter known as the offended. The wrongdoer admits he or she is wrong and asks for forgiveness. It's a risky venture, but once the wrongdoer has asked for forgiveness, he or she is freed from the chains of bitterness, regardless of the offended person's decision. Case closed.

Tom wasn't doing what God wanted him to do. And he knew it. Romans 12:18 says, "If possible, live in peace with everyone. Do that as much as you can." To live in peace with people, we have to forgive them. Forgiveness is a gift that God has given us and wants us to use with each other, even when it hurts or we don't feel like forgiving. Tom knew this.

But to say he forgave Richard would have been a lie. Instead of lying, Tom and Whit started to pray together so Tom would eventually be able to forgive Richard.

Daily Challenge

Think of someone you've hurt in some way. Go to that person, say you're sorry, and ask for forgiveness. These steps will help you as much as or more than they help the person you hurt.

• • •

Forgiveness Theme Memory Verse—Ephesians 4:32

Be kind and tender to one another. Forgive each other, just as God forgave you because of what Christ has done.

Devo 48

The Full Apology

Today's Verse—Acts 2:38

Peter replied, "All of you must turn away from your sins and be baptized in the name of Jesus Christ. Then your sins will be forgiven. You will receive the gift of the Holy Spirit."

"**S**orry, Mom!" called Jim as he hurried out the door. The living-room carpet was soggy, and bits of burst balloons were all over the floor.

Do you think what Jim said showed his mother he was truly sorry? (I don't either.) Sometimes a quick "I'm sorry" isn't enough. Let's rewind and start over.

"Sorry, Mom!" Jim said to his mother while looking into her eyes. "I threw water balloons in the living room." Then he hurried outside to play ball.

It's good Jim expressed that he was sorry and showed that he knew what he'd done wrong. But that wasn't enough either. Let's rewind and start over.

"Sorry, Mom!" said Jim, looking at his mother. "I threw water balloons in the living room when you told me not to. I made a mess."

Was adding regret to the apology enough? No. Let's rewind and start over.

"Sorry, Mom!" said Jim, looking at his mother. "I threw water balloons in the living room when you told me not to. I made a mess. Will you forgive me?"

Jim was getting close to a full apology. Let's rewind one last time.

"Sorry, Mom!" said Jim, looking at his mother. "I threw water balloons in the living room when you told me not to. I made a mess. Will you forgive me?" Then, instead of running outside like he wanted to, Jim helped her clean up the mess. He continued, "I won't throw water balloons in the house again. What can I do to make up for the time it's taken you to help me dry the carpet and clean the room?"

That was a full apology. Jim expressed his sorrow, showed he understood what

Wandering with Wooton

Have you ever thought how great it would be to have a GPS for your life? Instead of giving driving directions, it could say, "Don't say what you're thinking," or "Go over and help that person," so you'd never offend anyone for the rest of your life. I guess God's Holy Spirit is kind of like that. He's always directing us to do what's right. Amazing! That means we already have a Holy Spirit GPS, or HS-GPS!

he'd done, asked for forgiveness, said he wouldn't do it again, and made things right. Phew!

And next time, Jim will probably remember to take the water ballons outside. No rewind necessary.

Daily Challenge

What do you want to hear when someone apologizes to you? Find out how each person in your family likes to be apologized to. Then remember that for future reference.

• • •

Forgiveness Theme Memory Verse—Ephesians 4:32

Be kind and tender to one another. Forgive each other, just as God forgave you because of what Christ has done.

Devo 49

Running from Yourself

Today's Verse—1 John 2:12

Dear children, I'm writing to you because your sins have been forgiven. They have been forgiven because of what Jesus has done.

You're standing in a crowded street. The excitement grows. Today you'll test your running ability against a dozen stampeding bulls. You hear the first rocket. That means the corral gate has been opened. You run forward. The second rocket sounds. The bulls rush into the streets. You and the rest of the runners pick up speed.

With each step, you feel the danger. Others push ahead of you. You fall behind and can't get your footing. The small herd of snorting bulls charges toward you . . .

• • •

In some ways, the Running of the Bulls in Pamplona, Spain, is similar to a person running from self-forgiveness. When people can't forgive themselves, they take off running on the inside, but their guilt follows close behind, charging as if it were an angry bull.

Some people try to ignore their shame, but when they become weary of running, their unforgiving spirit can trample them. In the *Odyssey* episode "Welcome Home, Mr. Blackgaard" (album 26), Edwin Blackgaard thought the townspeople wouldn't forgive him because of what his brother had done to Odyssey. When Edwin found that they had forgiven him, he couldn't accept their kindness. Almost too late he realized that it wasn't the town that wouldn't forgive him. He hadn't forgiven himself.

God wants us to confess our sins to Him, ask others for forgiveness, and forgive ourselves. We need to give even our shame and guilt into His care. The apostle John said, "Dear children, I'm writing to you because your sins have been forgiven. They have been forgiven because of what Jesus has done" (1 John 2:12).

Whit and Wisdom

Forgiveness starts with God and continues through us. Just as He has forgiven us, we need to forgive others. When Peter asked Jesus how many times we must forgive, he thought he was being generous with forgiving seven times. Then Jesus corrected him and said seven times seventy (Matthew 18:21-22). In other words, Jesus suggested a much greater, even more ridiculous, amount. No amount is too high when it comes to forgiveness. If God kept a tally of our sins and allowed only an exact number of times He would forgive us, we'd be in big trouble. But He offers us forgiveness whenever we sincerely ask. He expects us to do the same for others every time we've been wronged.

Once you forgive yourself, the final rockets—the third and fourth ones—can be fired. In Spain this means that the Pamplona race is over. The bulls are where they need to be, a winner is declared, and the runners are free to go home.

Family Challenge #7—Popcorn Forgiveness

Make some popcorn for your family and then gather them together. Find an unpopped kernel and compare it to a popped one. Show how large a single kernel can become. Consider how not forgiving others can explode into relationship problems. As you eat the popcorn with your family, talk about how great God's gift of forgiveness is.

• • •

Forgiveness Theme Memory Verse—Ephesians 4:32

Be kind and tender to one another. Forgive each other, just as God forgave you because of what Christ has done.

Ephesians Fit-In

Place each of the **bold** words from Ephesians 1:7 in the puzzle. No word is repeated. (Repeat words are not in bold.) Fit all the words in this puzzle.

"We have been set free because of what Christ has done.
Through his blood our sins have been **forgiven.**
We have been set free because **God's grace is so rich"**
(Ephesians One: Seven).

Puzzle #7

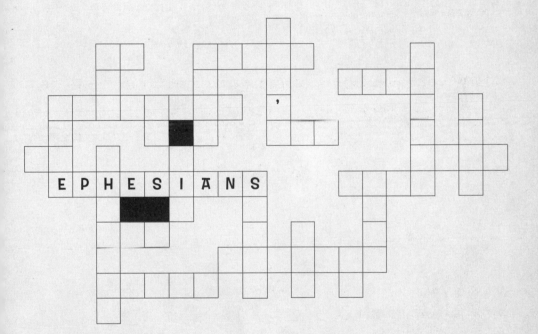

E P H E S I A N S

Answers on page 241.

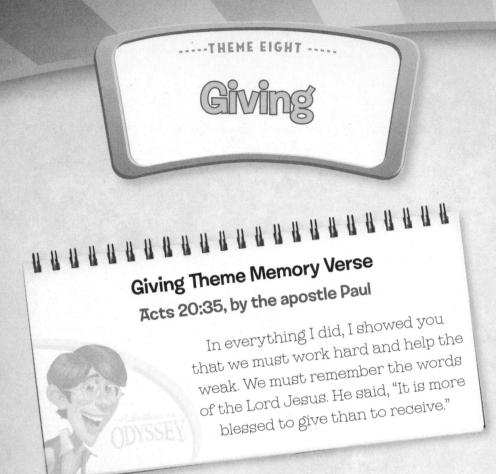

Giving Theme Memory Verse
Acts 20:35, by the apostle Paul

In everything I did, I showed you that we must work hard and help the weak. We must remember the words of the Lord Jesus. He said, "It is more blessed to give than to receive."

Can you relate to this kid who said, "Why is there a week of lessons about giving in this book? I'm ten years old. I get five dollars a week for my allowance. All my clothes are hand-me-downs from my older brother. In three years I'll hand my clothes down to my little brother. All of my toys are either my favorites, or they're broken (usually by my little brother) or have missing pieces. My parents buy just enough food for our family for the week, but nothing more. So I don't have anything to give!"

Do you feel the same way? Even if you don't have much, there are still many ways you can give. Giving is about more than just offering your stuff to people. Giving is an attitude. Giving is a lifestyle. And giving is a choice. You can decide to keep all of your stuff for yourself, or you can obey the commands of God and be generous with your possessions.

Jesus talked about giving to the poor all through the Gospels. He also talked about the alternative—greed. This week we'll explore what you can give, why you should give, and what the consequences are when you're greedy.

You'll probably find that you have more to give than you think.

Prayer

Dear God,

You have given me so much. It's all Yours. Help me to have a spirit of generosity to give what isn't really mine to begin with.

Amen.

Devo 50

In Rod We Trust?

Honor the Lord with your wealth.
Give him the first share of all your crops.

You have one dollar in your pocket. You're in church, and the service is almost over. You're really looking forward to taking that dollar to the vending machine and picking out a package of salted pretzel rods. You already know the vending machine code: D-5. You can already taste the buttery, salty, crunchy goodness . . . Without warning, the pastor calls the ushers to the front of the church. It's time for the offering! You're beginning to wonder if the pretzel-rod idea is wrong. *Should I put the dollar in the offering plate instead? Should I give the money to God?* You begin to sweat a little. Your breath becomes short and quick. The offering plate is coming closer . . . closer . . .

• • •

Before you make your decision, let's look at a story from John 6. It probably happened something like this. A boy from Galilee who joined a crowd following Jesus. Everyone was excited, pushing toward the hill where Jesus was. The boy had to stand on his tiptoes to see what was happening. He had heard stories about Jesus, the teacher who healed the sick and even cast out demons. He had come a long way to see what Jesus would do next. His mother had even packed him some food: five small loaves of bread and two fish.

It was getting late, and the people were hungry. Jesus' disciples must have noticed, because one of them came over and asked if anyone had any food. The boy looked at the huge crowd and then at his small basket. He had really been looking forward to his dinner that night. Besides, what good would five loaves and two fish do for all these people?

But the boy followed the disciple to the top of the hill. There, he gave Jesus his

Wandering with Wooton

I've been taught to *tithe*. This means giving 10 percent of everything I earn back to God. When I was young, I had a job where I earned a few bucks an hour. A tenth was giving up some licorice and maybe a sea monkey or two. As an adult I make a lot more money, and now it's giving up, like, *two hundred sea monkeys!* I'm just glad I got in the habit of giving 10 percent when I was young, or it would be really difficult now.

basket of food. Jesus took the five loaves of bread and two fish, and He miraculously multiplied them and fed all five thousand people or more (see Loquacious Learning with Eugene on page 27). There were even leftovers!

So have you made your decision about the pretzels yet? It probably isn't wrong to buy pretzels. But remember that Jesus has a way of taking what you give and multiplying it. He could fill big needs with your small amount of money.

So next week, bring extra money to church. The pretzels will still be in D-5.

Daily Challenge

Whatever you earn from your allowance, jobs, or chores, set aside a specific amount to give at church that week. Put it away or give it to your parents so you won't feel tempted to spend it before Sunday rolls around.

• • •

Giving Theme Memory Verse—Acts 20:35, by the apostle Paul

In everything I did, I showed you that we must work hard and help the weak. We must remember the words of the Lord Jesus. He said, "It is more blessed to give than to receive."

Devo 51

Mine!

Today's Verse—Hebrews 13:16

Don't forget to do good. Don't forget to share with others. God is pleased with those kinds of offerings.

Sharing comes naturally for all of us. You can tell when you look into the nursery class for two-year-olds at church. Peer into the room, and you'll see twenty-five young children living happily together, generously sharing their toys with each other . . .

"Hey, Timmy, can I borrow your teddy bear?"

"Sure, Johnny. But I would like it back before class ends."

"How about we take turns with the teddy?"

"Great idea."

Is that how two-year-olds behave? *No way!* This is how things *really* are in that nursery:

"Gimme that teddy!"

"Mine!"

"I'm taking it!"

"WAAAH!"

Sharing doesn't come naturally for us after all. We have our stuff, and we don't want anybody else using it. Sharing is something we all need to learn. In the *Odyssey* episode* "Share and Share Alike" (album 23), Jack Allen held a Share-a-Thon to raise money for the Odyssey shelter for the homeless, and Kids Radio presented three sketches to demonstrate why we should share. The first reason is because when we

---

* Did you know that almost every *Odyssey* episode has a lesson? You can find more episodes on biblical lessons like giving at *www.whitsend.org/vault*. Look for the area that says "Browse by Lesson."

Connie's Corner

I have this thing about my hair dryer. I know it's weird, but I don't like anybody using it. I have a roommate now, and she was always using it. So I started hiding it. But she kept finding it. So I hid it better. And now I can't find it. I probably would have been better off just sharing it.

share, others will want to share with us. The second reason is because nothing we own is actually ours. God has given us everything we have. So we need to be willing to share our things with others because they're actually God's property. The third reason we should share is because Jesus asks us to. He doesn't want us to put so much importance on our stuff that we forget about doing good to others.

If you're reading this book, you're probably not two years old. So you've probably been taught for a long time to share. Learn that lesson now. Some adults have yet to learn it, and most of them are miserable. There's great joy in being able to help others out by sharing with them what God has given you.

Daily Challenge

Offer something that's important to you to a little brother or sister, or if you don't have one, to a neighbor kid. Pick something that you don't like to share so that it's a sacrifice for you. It will get you into the good habit of sharing, even when you don't want to.

• • •

Giving Theme Memory Verse—Acts 20:35, by the apostle Paul

In everything I did, I showed you that we must work hard and help the weak. We must remember the words of the Lord Jesus. He said, "It is more blessed to give than to receive."

Devo 52

Generosity

You should each give what you have decided in your heart to give. You shouldn't give if you don't want to. You shouldn't give because you are forced to. God loves a cheerful giver.

Brian Kluth, author of the best-selling book *You Are Invited on a 40 Day Spiritual Journey to a More Generous Life,* was interviewed by NBC television. The reporter asked him, "So, do you think God wants everyone rich?"

Kluth said, "No, I don't believe that."

The reporter said, "Then what do you believe?"

Kluth responded, "I believe that everyone needs to learn to become more generous with whatever God has given them."

"Well, didn't your book becoming a best seller make you rich?"

Kluth said, "No, it helped me become more generous!"

The Bible says that "God loves a cheerful giver" (2 Corinthians 9:7). Brian Kluth is obviously one of those.

• • •

To serve Jesus with all of our hearts, we must not put our "stuff" ahead of Him. We must have a spirit of generosity. In the *Odyssey* episode "For Three Dollars More" (album 56), Barrett wondered what good his three dollars were going to do if he gave it to the church. Three dollars couldn't build a new children's wing at the church. It couldn't send a missionary to Africa.

What Barrett learned is that giving money isn't just about helping the church or missionaries. It's about developing a spirit of generosity and getting into the habit of giving. It's about acquiring the desire to help others who are less fortunate than we are.

Loquacious Learning with Eugene

Surveys consistently find that 65 to 85 percent of all American adults give to charitable organizations and that the average American gives around $1,900 per year to charity. Giving to others, whether through a church or a charity, is a way to show that we understand the value of sharing.

Giving isn't a natural thing. We have to be taught—or we have to teach ourselves. But a spirit of generosity is so much better than a spirit of greed.

Daily Challenge

This week, give over and above what you would normally give to church or to others. Find some change in the couch cushions, or shake a little out of your piggy bank. Be generous!

• • •

Giving Theme Memory Verse—Acts 20:35, by the apostle Paul

In everything I did, I showed you that we must work hard and help the weak. We must remember the words of the Lord Jesus. He said, "It is more blessed to give than to receive."

Devo 53

God, the Provider

Today's Verse—Philippians 4:19

My God will meet all your needs. He will meet
them in keeping with his wonderful riches
that come to you because you belong to Christ Jesus.

Tears welled up in Stephanie's eyes as she listened to a man talk about missions work he was doing in Guatemala. Her heart went out to the children there who were living in poverty. The man gave out an address in case anyone wanted to send money to the missionaries there. Stephanie pulled out her checkbook. She knew she couldn't afford to give, but she began to write a check for twenty-five dollars.

Suddenly she felt in her heart that God was telling her to give more. She and her husband couldn't afford twenty-five dollars, much less fifty, but still she felt compelled to give more. So she wrote a check for fifty dollars. They might have to skip a few meals.

Months later, a missionary from Guatemala visited their church. Stephanie had no idea who this person was, but the man told the story about how, months earlier, the brakes on their Jeep went out, and they couldn't get supplies to the Guatemalan children. They prayed, and that very day, they received fifty dollars from a donor they had never met. They got the brakes fixed. The cost? Fifty dollars!

Not only had God provided for the Guatemalan children, but He had also provided for Stephanie and her family. They didn't have to skip meals that week, nor have they ever had to since.

• • •

In the book of 1 Kings, a widow in the town of Zarephath made her last meal for herself and her son. There was a famine in the land, and she had only enough flour for one more loaf of bread. She figured they would eat one last time, and die. But then

Wandering with Wooton

After reading that story in the Bible about Elijah and the widow, I decided to try it myself. I used a bunch of flour and made bread. Then I prayed that I would have more flour in the morning. It didn't work, but I kept on baking. After two weeks, I never got miracle flour, but I did get fourteen loaves of bread. So I took them to poor families in my neighborhood. I guess God blessed me after all!

a prophet of God named Elijah came to her and asked her for food. What nerve! The man was asking her to use her last bit of flour to feed him instead of her son? But he assured her that the flour wouldn't run out. She believed this man of God and did as he asked. She made him the bread, and he ate. When she went back into the house, she discovered that the flour jar was full again. (See 1 Kings 17:7–16.)

How has God kept your "flour jar" filled to the brim? He will bless you in surprising ways when you trust Him.

Daily Challenge

Take a step of faith and give more than you think you can give this week. Give money, food, clothing, or toys to a charity or to someone you know who is in need. God will bless you.

• • •

Giving Theme Memory Verse—Acts 20:35, by the apostle Paul

In everything I did, I showed you that we must work hard and help the weak. We must remember the words of the Lord Jesus. He said, "It is more blessed to give than to receive."

Devo 54

Greed

Today's Verse—1 Timothy 6:10

Love for money causes all kinds of evil. Some people want to get rich. They have wandered away from the faith. They have wounded themselves with many sorrows.

Welcome back to everybody's favorite game show *Box O' Cash*.

"Okay, George, it's up to you. You have one Box O' Cash left to open. If you choose to open it, you could walk away with a million dollars, or you could walk away with $1.25. If you choose not to open it, you get to keep your money. You leave with $500,000. What are you gonna do?"

The crowd cheers and hollers to urge George on.

"Oh, Roy, this is big. If I walk away now, I get $500,000."

"That's right."

"But I could try for the million."

"You got it. Of course, you could also walk away with $1.25."

"Oh, Roy . . . I really want that million. Open that Box O' Cash!"

The crowd goes crazy.

• • •

Are you kidding me? Why would anybody risk half a million dollars?

Greed is about never being satisfied with what you have. And that means never. If you're a greedy person, and you end up getting the million dollars you want so badly, it won't be enough. You'll want two million. The world is filled with people who are miserable because they just can't get enough. Yet they've never known the joy of giving.

Jesus had a lot to say about greed. In Luke 12:15 He said, "Watch out! Be on your

138

Connie's Corner

One time I was tempted to quit my job at Whit's End because a friend told me I could make more money working at a department store. I thought about it for a while. Sure, the money was better, but I would be losing friendships, opportunities to talk to kids, and a wonderful job. Not a very good trade. I stayed at Whit's End instead. And, hey, the ice cream is better.

guard against wanting to have more and more things. Life is not made up of how much a person has."

Don't let greed keep you from giving. The joy you'll feel in giving will be far greater than the joy you'll feel in having more money than you need.

Daily Challenge

Make two lists—one of ten things you want that money can buy (a new bike, a video game, etc.), and one of ten things you want that money can't buy (friendships, respect, etc.). Compare the lists and decide which would be better.

• • •

Giving Theme Memory Verse—Acts 20:35, by the apostle Paul

In everything I did, I showed you that we must work hard and help the weak. We must remember the words of the Lord Jesus. He said, "It is more blessed to give than to receive."

Devo 55

Other Stuff to Give

Today's Verse—1 Peter 4:10

God's gifts of grace come in many forms.
Each of you has received a gift in order to
serve others. You should use it faithfully.

Rich Mullins was a giver. He was a Christian singer who was very popular in the 1980s and 1990s. His song "Awesome God" was sung in pretty much every evangelical church in America during those decades, and still is popular today. Even though he was an extremely talented singer and songwriter, he never considered his singing to be his most important ministry. He sang to pay the bills.

Instead, his ministry was showing God's love by helping and serving others. He took a vow of poverty, which meant he would never accept more money than he needed. His music sold like crazy, but he never had any idea how well. He never wanted to know. All of the money that came in for his songs and concerts went to charity. He accepted only a small church salary, and during the final years of his life, he taught music to children on a Navajo reservation.

Not only did Mullins give his money to God; he also gave his time and talents to Him. You also have more to give away than just your money. You have talents that God desires to use. Your job is to figure out how to use them to help others.

Even people without obvious talents can still give of their time. Can you mow lawns? Rake leaves? Shovel snow? Make cookies? You can do all of these things for your neighbors, friends, or even total strangers. Does your church need any volunteers to watch babies in the nursery? Set up chairs? Wash dishes after a fellowship dinner? If you keep your eyes open, you'll see plenty of ways to serve God.

Loquacious Learning with Eugene

School-aged children get an average of 9.5 hours of sleep per day. Assuming a school week of 35 hours, that leaves 3,990 waking minutes in one week. If you subtract a mere one hour per week, that would still leave 3,930 minutes for eating, playing, attending to homework, and various other activities. An hour set aside per week would be an excellent amount to use to start serving others.

Daily Challenge

Do some chores for no money. Do something for your neighbors and don't expect anything back. Make them some cookies or a cake. Even better, do something in secret, like leaving a basket of flowers on the doorstep. Bless somebody's day.

• • •

Giving Theme Memory Verse—Acts 20:35, by the apostle Paul

In everything I did, I showed you that we must work hard and help the weak. We must remember the words of the Lord Jesus. He said, "It is more blessed to give than to receive."

Devo 56

Giving When It Hurts

Today's Verse—Psalm 4:5

Offer sacrifices to the Lord in the right way. Trust in him.

Joe the Pharisee was pretty proud of himself. He walked into the temple with a huge bag of coins. He knew this would be impressive. As he reached the offering box, he peered around him to see who was looking.

Everyone. Good.

He pulled out his coins. "Augh!" he said with some serious exaggeration to show its heft. Instead of dumping the entire bag at once, he decided to take out the coins one by one. That way everyone would see that he wasn't just giving small copper coins. These were denarii! A whole day's wages.

He placed each coin in the box until the entire bag was empty. He looked around at all the impressed people and then went to the back of the temple with his head held high.

Then an old widow walked in. She wore raggedy clothes and sandals that were falling apart. This was a woman who had practically nothing. She shuffled slowly to the offering box and raised her hand. Out fell two copper coins, which were worth about a penny.

Joe scoffed quietly. Two copper coins! Pathetic!

Jesus, who was standing behind Joe, began talking to His disciples. Joe eavesdropped. Jesus said, "What I'm about to tell you is true. That poor widow has put more into the offering box than all the others."

What? Joe thought. *Didn't He see how much I put in?*

Jesus went on. "They all gave a lot because they are rich. But she gave even though she is poor. She put in everything she had. She gave all she had to live on." (See Mark 12:41–44.)

Joe walked away, sulking.

Whit and Wisdom

"It is more blessed to give than to receive" (Acts 20:35). It sounds like a nice little proverb, but it's often hard to put into practice. We love receiving presents at Christmas or on our birthdays. It's harder to reach into your pocket and take out that money we hope to spend on what we want and give it to someone else for what <u>they</u> need. The phrase "give until it hurts" is an accurate one for giving sacrificially. And yet, according to the Bible, that kind of giving brings greater blessing in the long run than indulging ourselves. Try giving up your time, your belongings, or your money to others and see what happens!

Family Challenge #8—Giving Game

Decide as a family how you can give. Make a list of things you can give away. Then make a list of things you can do to serve your community, your church, your extended family, or your neighbors. Have a bake sale or a car wash, or put up a stand and sell lemonade. Then give all the proceeds to the charity of your choice. It'll be a great way to spend a day with your family, and it's a wonderful way to serve God!

• • •

Giving Theme Memory Verse—Acts 20:35, by the apostle Paul

In everything I did, I showed you that we must work hard and help the weak. We must remember the words of the Lord Jesus. He said, "It is more blessed to give than to receive."

Giving Word Search

Find these words in the grid:

BLESSINGS   JOY

CHARITY   PROVIDE

CHEERFUL   SHARING

GENEROSITY   TIME

GIVE   TITHE

GREED   TRUST

Puzzle #8

```
H C E T D O X J F U A T P Y T
B L E S S I N G S D G R T G S
C Y T I R A H C O I O I Y O U
D H G U M D J F K V S G F C R
L E E I E V O M I O H D Y E T
F N E E V P Y D R U A Y H Q O
H T R R R E E E G D R T S N U
N P Y S G F N O M Q I T I M E
Q V T R I E U P C T N X A B V
W M O V G S T L U I G B L K J
N P X P C O F D B A T B B V G
Z E D N T P A T Q I Z R P F B
P Z F X Q E X K R T G F Z X Q
T O X B N G X U K U D Y L G E
S U O N L X P I F A C S S U H
```

Answers on page 242.

Witnessing Theme Memory Verse
Matthew 28:19–20

[Jesus said,] "You must go and make disciples of all nations. Baptize them in the name of the Father and of the Son and of the Holy Spirit. Teach them to obey everything I have commanded you. And you can be sure that I am always with you, to the very end."

"**O**h, man! I can't wait to tell Jordan about . . ."

How do you think that sentence ends?

". . . the dress I bought!"

". . . what happened at Jeremy's party!"

". . . the concert!"

". . . those great-tasting sourdough bagels at the bakery!"

It might not even occur to you to say ". . . Jesus!" But if you think about it, why not? You have the best news anyone could ever hear. Jesus loves everyone and is waiting to be their Savior. But you might not always be excited about telling people this good news. Why not?

Witnessing means sharing Jesus with others. It's telling your friends, family, and neighbors about the person who saved you. Jesus wants to be a part of their lives, too.

Witnessing can be hard because you may not think you have the right words to say. Or you may be afraid that people are going to think you're a freak. But just like Bible study, prayer, and worship, witnessing is one of the things Christians need to do to stay in a healthy relationship with Jesus. Jesus even commanded it. In Matthew 28:19–20, He said, "You must go and make disciples of all nations. Baptize them in the name of the Father and of the Son and of the Holy Spirit. Teach them to obey everything I have commanded you."

This week, we're going to talk about witnessing. Why is it important? What words can you use to tell people about Jesus? And should witnessing be about more than the words you say?

Hopefully by the end of the week, you'll be as excited to tell people about Jesus as you were about those sourdough bagels.

Prayer

Dear God,

Thank You for my salvation. Help me to be willing to share the joy I've felt in knowing You. Help me tell others about You.

Amen.

Devo
57

The Words of Life

Today's Verse—Romans 1:1

I, Paul, am writing this letter. I serve Christ Jesus.
I have been appointed to be an apostle.
God set me apart to tell others his good news.

China wasn't a pleasant place to live in the 1800s. But this is where Lottie Moon chose to go. She was a missionary to China when war, famine, disease, and extreme poverty were the norm. The hardships were exactly the reasons why Lottie felt called to China. Who needs to hear more about the God of hope than people who are hopeless?

Lottie lived among the Chinese people, and she was accepted as one of their own. She repeatedly asked the Foreign Missions Board for more money to help her and the Chinese people. She also pleaded for them to send more missionaries to China to tell the Chinese about Jesus. The board responded positively. Eventually a Christmas offering was begun to help foreign missionaries around the world. Today the fund is still called the Lottie Moon Christmas Offering, and more than $1.5 billion has been raised since 1888.

In that era, churches and mission boards really frowned upon single women becoming missionaries to dangerous countries like China. But none of that stopped Lottie. She said, "How can I help but speak when I have the words of life?"

You have the words of life too. You know what it means to be a Christian. You know that Jesus offers wonderful things like peace, joy, purpose, and love. You also know people who argue and fight with others and don't have peace. You know miserable people who have no joy. You know people who seem to be wandering around without any purpose for their lives. And you know people who feel unloved.

Connie's Corner

I'm a big "recommender." I recommend things all the time. Last week I told twelve people to try white-chocolate-chip ice cream. I told three people to see the movie *Unbroken Hearts* (take some tissues). But I don't recommend church to people often enough. Or Jesus. And Jesus is way better than ice cream. Or a movie. I probably need to change that.

You know about heaven and the wonderful gift salvation offers. You know people who don't know whether they will go to heaven one day. You probably even know people who don't believe in heaven.

If you know what you know, and you know people who don't know what you know, then the question is . . .

How can *you* not speak to others when you have the words of life?

Daily Challenge

Make a list of people you feel are missing out on the great blessings of being a Christian. Remember people who seem sad or lonely or angry. Begin to pray for them.

• • •

Witnessing Theme Memory Verse—Matthew 28:19–20

[Jesus said,] "You must go and make disciples of all nations. Baptize them in the name of the Father and of the Son and of the Holy Spirit. Teach them to obey everything I have commanded you. And you can be sure that I am always with you, to the very end."

Devo 58

Earning Your Right to Speak

Today's Verse—1 Peter 2:12

People who don't believe might say you are doing wrong. But lead good lives among them. Then they will see your good works. And they will give glory to God.

You're having trouble with history class. All those dates and names and wars and treaties are killing you. A few days before an exam, you see an ad in the school newspaper that reads, "History Tutor: $3.00 an hour. Call Edward Tanner." The ad also gives a phone number.

You think this ad sounds like a good deal. Three dollars an hour isn't bad. If you study with this kid for three hours, and for less than ten bucks, you can get an A on the history test. You've never met Edward, but Edwards are usually smart, right? So you give him a call, and you agree to meet with him at the library after school.

At the library he introduces himself, and he seems like a nice guy. You take out your history book and put it on a study table. He reaches into his bag and pulls out some papers. You happen to notice a piece of paper on the top. It's a history test with the name Edward Tanner on it. And written in bright red ink underneath is "43% F."

When Edward goes to the restroom, you take a closer look at the test. One of the questions is "What was the Gettysburg Address?" and his answer is "1313 Gettysburg Road."

When Edward gets back to the study table, you quickly say, "You know, I don't

Wandering with Wooton

There's this one guy on my mail route who didn't know about Jesus. One day he said to me, "How come you never stop to talk to me like you do with Mrs. Randolph?" I wanted to say, "Because your pet bird gives me the evil eye," but I didn't. I felt bad. I realized I need to be friends with this guy. Maybe soon he'll listen when I talk to him about Jesus.

think I need to study anymore." You plop down a dollar for twenty minutes of study time and run out of the library as fast as you can.

• • •

Why would you let a bad history student teach you history? In the same way, why would people want to hear about Christianity from you if they see you doing things that aren't Christian? Telling people about Jesus is important, but it's just as important to live like Jesus. When people see Christ in you, they are far more likely to listen to you when you start telling them about Jesus.

Daily Challenge

Take out the list of people you made yesterday. Pick somebody on the list and do something nice for him or her.

• • •

Witnessing Theme Memory Verse—Matthew 28:19-20

[Jesus said,] "You must go and make disciples of all nations. Baptize them in the name of the Father and of the Son and of the Holy Spirit. Teach them to obey everything I have commanded you. And you can be sure that I am always with you, to the very end."

Devo 59

How to Witness

Today's Verse—Mark 1:17

"Come. Follow me," Jesus said. "I will make you fishers of people."

In the *Odyssey* episode "Go Ye Therefore" (album 4), Connie Kendall was determined to witness to the world. She wanted to tell everyone about Jesus—friends, acquaintances, total strangers. No one was safe from being hit with a gospel water droplet from Connie's evangelism sprinkler.

But she had a problem. She didn't know how to tell people about Jesus. She tried everything! First she tried handing out Christian pamphlets. But she got snubbed. Then she tried putting the pamphlets inside books at the bookstore. But she got kicked out. Then she tried plastering Christian bumper stickers all over her mother's car. Her mother wasn't too happy.

Finally she decided to be bold at school. She began telling her friends at a study-hall table that their lives were empty. They just laughed at her. As it turned out, though, one of the girls at the table was impressed enough to seek Connie out later. The girl asked Connie why she was so joyful all the time. Connie got a chance to witness about Jesus after all.

• • •

The thing is, there isn't just one way to witness. Bring up your faith in natural ways. Explain why you feel so strongly about church or prayer or reading your Bible. If people know you're a Christian, and they see that your life is something special, they'll be naturally curious about what makes you tick. Being a witness with your life is an especially effective tool. (You'll read about that later in the week. You'll also learn how to use your personal story to witness to others.)

Loquacious Learning with Eugene

Statistics show that 77 percent of all Christians made their decision for Jesus before their twenty-first birthday. That's precisely why God needs children to reach their friends for Christ. Once people become adults, they are less likely to ever make that decision. Don't make the mistake of believing that witnessing is simply the pastor's job or an adult's job. Jesus calls us all to be "fishers of people."

If you get to the point where one of your friends wants to make a decision for Jesus, you can ask a Sunday school teacher, pastor, or parent to help you. Or you can lead your friend in the salvation prayer from devotion 5 ("What Must I Do to Be Saved?") in this book.

However you do it, be sincere, be loving, and be excited to share your faith in Jesus with others.

Daily Challenge

Remember that list you made two days ago that you took out yesterday? Take it out again. Find someone on that list that you can invite to church or to a church activity. Keep praying for those people too.

• • •

Witnessing Theme Memory Verse—Matthew 28:19-20

[Jesus said,] "You must go and make disciples of all nations. Baptize them in the name of the Father and of the Son and of the Holy Spirit. Teach them to obey everything I have commanded you. And you can be sure that I am always with you, to the very end."

Devo
60

Your Personal Testimony

Today's Verse—1 Peter 3:15

Always be ready to give an answer to anyone who asks you about the hope you have.

A man once spent 163 hours trapped under a refrigerator . . . and lived to tell about it! He was moving his refrigerator to clean underneath it, and it toppled over on him. It was far too heavy to move, and he couldn't reach his cell phone. He lived alone in a house in the country, so his neighbors were far away. They couldn't hear his cries of pain. For the next few days, he lay there on the kitchen floor. Fortunately, he was able to pull the refrigerator door open a little bit and get some food. He ate lots of cheese, sliced meats, and butter, since those were in the door of the refrigerator. Yes, he was desperate enough to eat plain butter.

Even worse than the pain of being trapped and the boredom of being still, he felt empty. After a week he figured he was going to die there. No one would even notice he was gone. He realized that his life had no purpose.

Suddenly a light shone through the window and formed a cross on the ceiling. The man gave his life to Jesus right then. Not a minute after he prayed, his cow, Bessie, broke through the back door and pushed the refrigerator off of him. He was free. In more ways than one.

• • •

Okay, that wasn't a true story. But have you ever heard one of these crazy, unbelievable testimonies from somebody? Do you ever wish you had a great story that would make telling people about Jesus easier?

Connie's Corner

Growing up in California, I wasn't a criminal, a bad student, or a troublemaker. But my life was heading in the wrong direction. When I came to Odyssey, Whit introduced me to Jesus. And since I respected Whit, I began to respect Jesus. Whit led me to Christ, and I've never been the same since. It's amazing how much real joy and purpose you find once Jesus means everything to you.

Your story may be better than you think. Jesus is working in your life in ways that you may not even see. Think about it. How does Jesus change the decisions you make? Do you feel more joy, peace, or patience because of Jesus? How has He changed the way you look at life, at your family, at the future?

People will respond to your story about the God who gives you hope. People can cast doubts about Jesus. They can cast doubts about the Bible. But a personal story about how Jesus makes your life beautiful is something no one can debate.

Daily Challenge

Write out your personal story about how you came to believe in Jesus. Be sure to include statements like "Because of Jesus, I'm different in the way I . . ." Or "Because of having Jesus in my life, I feel . . ." Or "Jesus makes my life better because . . ."

• • •

Witnessing Theme Memory Verse—Matthew 28:19-20

[Jesus said,] "You must go and make disciples of all nations. Baptize them in the name of the Father and of the Son and of the Holy Spirit. Teach them to obey everything I have commanded you. And you can be sure that I am always with you, to the very end."

Devo 61

That Guy

Today's Verse—Matthew 5:16

In the same way, let your light shine in front of others. Then they will see the good things you do. And they will praise your Father who is in heaven.

Aman walks down a red carpet wearing a four-thousand-dollar suit. A crowd screams when he looks in their direction. He gives a quick wave, and teenage girls faint. These people have waited in line for twelve hours to get a sixty-second glance at a man who made seventeen million dollars working two months on a movie.

The actor's muscles have been toned with the help of the world's greatest trainers. His teeth have been whitened by a rare liquid that comes only from the sweat of the endangered Big-headed Amazon River Turtle. He has a website that gets three hundred thousand hits a day, and he hasn't updated it in six months. He is respected, loved, and envied by all living creatures. Anyone who takes one glance at this man will say, like everyone else on the planet . . . "I want to be like that guy!"

God wants you to be like that movie star. Well, sort of. He wants you to be a person others want to imitate. In the *Odyssey* episode* "The Holy Hoopster" (album 56), Ryan Cummings decided to use his school basketball career as an opportunity to thank Jesus in front of others. His words made people think about prayer and Jesus. People criticized him for talking about Jesus, especially when his team lost or he played poorly. But the two things people couldn't criticize was how hard he worked to be the best basketball player he could be, and how he lived his life as an honorable

---

* Did you know there's behind-the-scenes information about current shows like this one? For example, you can hear a podcast interview with Adam Wylie, the voice of Ryan Cummings. Just visit *www.whitsend.org/podcast* and search for "Ryan Cummings" or "Adam Wylie."

Wandering with Wooton

A few years ago I won Mailman of the Year. It was strange because I'm not the best mailman. I'm slower than most of my coworkers. But the customers voted, and a lot of people voted for me. I guess it's because I talk to most of them. They know that I like them. I'm more interested in loving people than I am with being the fastest mailman. It may be bad for my career, but it's probably good for my witness.

person. He was a role model even if he wasn't the best basketball player.

If people see the fruits of your spirit—your love, your joy, your patience—they will want the same things for themselves. That's a great witness. Who knows, when you walk by, people may even say . . .

"I want to be like that guy!"

Daily Challenge

Think of a time when you have been a poor example of the person Jesus wants you to be. Think of a time when you did this in front of someone. Make it a point to go to that person today, apologize for your behavior, and think of ways to ensure you don't repeat the mistake.

• • •

Witnessing Theme Memory Verse—Matthew 28:19-20

[Jesus said,] "You must go and make disciples of all nations. Baptize them in the name of the Father and of the Son and of the Holy Spirit. Teach them to obey everything I have commanded you. And you can be sure that I am always with you, to the very end."

Devo
62

Missionaries to Main Street

Today's Verse—Acts 1:8

[Jesus said,] "You will receive power when the Holy Spirit comes on you. Then you will be my witnesses in Jerusalem. You will be my witnesses in all Judea and Samaria. And you will be my witnesses from one end of the earth to the other."

Have you ever seen a Bible map with the apostle Paul's missionary journeys on it? It's ridiculous! There are usually three lines—one blue, one red, one green—marking Paul's first, second, and third missionary journeys. And the lines crisscross and double up and form pretzel-like routes. Paul went everywhere!

Doesn't that make you want to go somewhere? When you see pictures and video of people starving in Africa, Asia, and other places, don't you want to do something to help? So many of these people have no hope, and they don't know about Jesus. It's easy to think that the need over there is far greater than it is here in the United States.

Alex wanted to travel around the world in the *Odyssey* episode "Missionary: Impossible" (album 35). He wanted to be a missionary and immediately thought the first thing he should do was find appropriate African clothes. But Jason taught him that the first thing he needed to do was develop a heart for people and understand what it means to share Jesus with people.

Having dreams of being a missionary to a far-off place is wonderful. God may very well be leading you to Africa or somewhere else. A great way to get prepared for that journey is to become a missionary at home first. There are so many people in your own neighborhood who don't know about Jesus. There are so many people in your neigh-

Loquacious Learning with Eugene

A recent survey showed that 33 percent of all Americans hadn't attended any church in the previous six months. That's about one hundred million Americans. It's safe to assume that many of these people have no relationship with Jesus. What Jesus said in Matthew 9:37 is certainly true: "The harvest is huge. But there are only a few workers." God needs laborers.

borhood, or in the neighborhoods a few miles away, who have needs that you can fill with God's help. Those are things you can do right now.

Learn how to first serve your community. Then get your plane ticket to Africa.

Daily Challenge

For fun, make a missionary map for yourself. Chart the places around your town (or around the country) where you could do the work of Christ. Mark down where you could help out your community, feed the poor, or tell people about Jesus. Look for spots where you can make a difference. Make plans to impact the community in at least two places.

• • •

Witnessing Theme Memory Verse—Matthew 28:19-20

[Jesus said,] "You must go and make disciples of all nations. Baptize them in the name of the Father and of the Son and of the Holy Spirit. Teach them to obey everything I have commanded you. And you can be sure that I am always with you, to the very end."

Devo 63

Looking for Opportunities

Today's Verse—Colossians 4:5

Be wise in the way you act toward outsiders.
Make the most of every opportunity.

Philip was having a blast in Samaria. He preached about Christ and performed a few miracles, and as a result, lots of people came to know Jesus as their Savior. He had folks lined up all along the banks of the river to be baptized. They followed him everywhere to hear his message. What a great ministry he had in Samaria.

Then a strange thing happened. The Bible tells us that an angel spoke to Philip. "Go south to the desert road," he said. "It's the road that goes down from Jerusalem to Gaza" (Acts 8:26).

Perhaps for a few moments Philip wondered why God would want him to leave Samaria. He was having such a great impact there. Why go to Gaza? However, the Bible says that Philip just up and went.

On the way, Philip met with an Ethiopian official sitting in his chariot. Philip saw that he was reading the book of Isaiah. So Philip asked the Ethiopian if he understood what he was reading. The official said no. Philip explained that the Bible passage was talking about Jesus. The man made a decision to follow Christ right then and there. In fact, he got out of his chariot, and Philip baptized him in the water alongside the road.

Opportunities to share your faith are everywhere. If an opportunity arises to talk to someone about Jesus, there's a good chance that God led you to that place at that exact time. Don't pass it up.

Whit and Wisdom

Sometimes I teach older children in Sunday school, and they laugh at me when I make them sing the song "This Little Light of Mine." I suppose they feel childish holding up their fingers like candles and singing, "This little light of mine, I'm gonna let it shine. Let it shine, let it shine, let it shine!"

I think that simple song holds a great truth about sharing our faith with others. Jesus said that we are to be lights (Matthew 5:14-16), because He is the Light of the World (John 8:12).

Family Challenge #9—Love Lists

Have everyone in your family make lists of people you know who don't know Jesus as their Savior. Then compare your lists. Some people may be on more than one list. Relatives may be on many of the lists. Make it a point to pray for these people as a family. Show the love of Christ to them and help them with whatever problems they may have. Call them frequently. And be prepared to share Jesus with them.

• • •

Witnessing Theme Memory Verse—Matthew 28:19–20

[Jesus said,] "You must go and make disciples of all nations. Baptize them in the name of the Father and of the Son and of the Holy Spirit. Teach them to obey everything I have commanded you. And you can be sure that I am always with you, to the very end."

Puzzle #9

Witnessing Crossword

Across

1. Great missionary.
5. Try not to get trapped under one of these.
8. Foreign missionary Lottie _____.
10. This will give you power and wisdom when you witness. (two words)
12. Baptized an Ethiopian.

Down

2. You are the _____ of the world.
3. _____ your right to be heard.
4. Galatians 5 lists the _____ of the Spirit.
6. Make the most of these.
7. Your personal _____ is a good way to witness.
9. Matthew 28:19 tells us to make these.
11. 100 million Americans haven't gone here in six months.

Puzzle #9

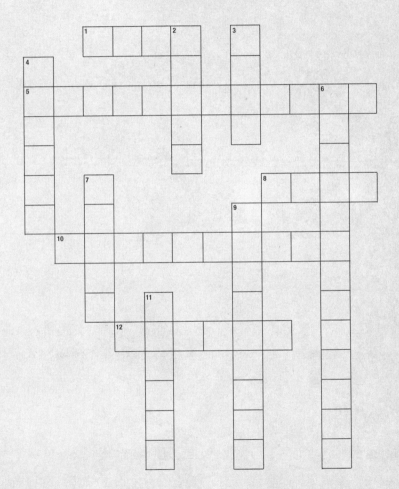

Answers on page 242.

Worship

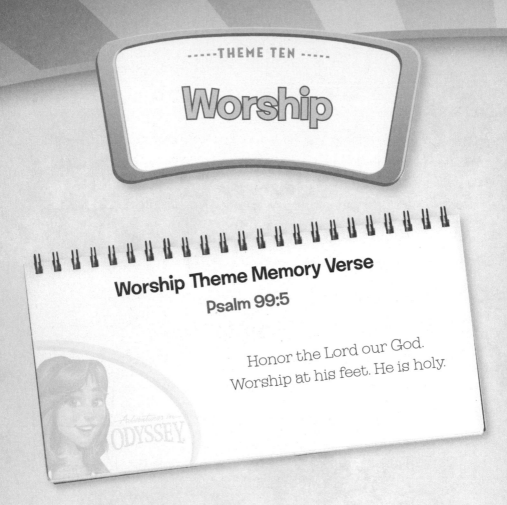

Worship Theme Memory Verse
Psalm 99:5

Honor the Lord our God.
Worship at his feet. He is holy.

Adventures in
ODYSSEY

I t would be wonderful if our country won a great battle against our enemies. But what if afterward the president himself stripped down to his boxers, danced in the streets of Washington, DC, and shouted, "Hooray to God!"?

You might call that silly, but the Bible would call it *worship*.

King David was so excited about winning a battle against the Philistines that he danced in the streets wearing only an apron. Amazingly, a whole crowd of Israelites danced with him. It was a glorious day. (See 2 Samuel 5:17–6:15.)

What other ways to worship are mentioned in the Bible? Why should we worship? Does worship mean we have to sit quietly and fold our hands at church?

This week we'll look at what worship is and find out just how great it can be. Be ready to be surprised with what the Bible says about worship. (And remember, before you can dance in the streets in a loincloth like King David did, you'll have to ask your mom *and* slay a bunch of Philistines.)

Prayer

Dear God,

This week open my mind so that I understand why You want Your people to worship You. Teach me how to worship You from my heart.

Amen.

Devo 64

Ways to Worship

Today's Verse—Psalm 109:30

With my mouth I will continually praise the Lord.
I will praise him when all of his people gather for worship.

Ellen loves worship. She loves singing hymns of praise to God. She loves the sounds of the choir, the passionate prayers, the moments of silent adoration for the God who loves her. But most of all, she loves it when she hears those poetic, powerful words fill the entire building . . .

"Canned ham is now buy one, get one free in aisle five."

What? Wait a minute! Ellen is in the grocery store?

When we think of worship, most of the time we think about sitting in church. But did you know that worship can happen anywhere? Ellen finds that she can worship anywhere, even while shopping. She can sing songs in her head, pray short prayers in her mind, and worship God while in the produce section. Worship is honoring God for who He is and what He has done. And you can do that anywhere!

Do you also know that worship isn't just singing? You can honor God by reading His Word. In the Bible God shows you who He is and what He wants you to do. Studying God's thoughts on a subject is another way of worshipping Him.

You can honor God by giving your tithes and offerings. When you give, you show God that you love Him more than money. You also honor Him when you obey His commands by giving to help churches, charities, and people who don't have much themselves.

You can honor God by listening to Him and obeying Him. You honor Him by teaching others about Him. You honor Him by thinking about Him, no matter where you are.

Loquacious Learning with Eugene

Worship services in ancient times used a vast array of musical instruments. The Bible speaks of the timbrel, which is similar to the modern tambourine. The sistrum was a metal stick with a hoop and rods at the end. When shaken like a rattle, it created a pleasant clanking sound. Whether instruments like these, an organ, or an electric guitar are used, God appreciates worship through music.

You can worship God by bowing, standing, kneeling, or dancing, with your hands raised, to your side, or folded in front of you. It doesn't matter, as long as you "worship the Father in spirit and in truth" (John 4:23). Your worship should be sincere and from the heart.

Wherever you are and whatever you're doing, God wants your worship so that you're always thinking about Him.

And, for goodness' sake, get to aisle five! That's a great sale on canned ham!

Daily Challenge

Find the courage to sing a praise song to God, maybe even in public (gasp!).

• • •

Worship Theme Memory Verse—Psalm 99:5

Honor the Lord our God. Worship at his feet. He is holy.

Devo 65

Nuts About P-Nut

Today's Verse—Psalm 30:12

So my heart will sing to you. I can't keep silent.
Lord, my God, I will give you thanks forever.

Imagine your excitement. Your favorite singer of all time is coming to your town—pop sensation P-Nut!

His limousine pulls up. The crowd around you goes wild! He steps out—and walks directly toward you! He locks eyes with you. He steps up and reaches out his hand to shake yours. And the first words out of your mouth are . . .

"Nice to meet you. I wonder what's on TV." Or . . .

"Nice to meet you. I think I'm gonna get Chinese food for lunch." Or . . .

"Oops! That's my cell phone. It's a call from the dog groomer. Excuse me. Gotta take this."

Of course not! No, your first words to P-Nut will be praise for how much you adore his music, or compliments on his last album, or simply the words "I love you!"

• • •

Every day you have the opportunity to come into the presence of God. He is the One who created the universe. He gave you life. He is merciful, holy, and powerful. He gave up His Son for you. But how often do you get up in the morning and waste a perfectly good chance to tell Him how much He means to you?

In the *Odyssey* episode* "Sunday Morning Scramble" (album 43), the Washington family was in such a frenzy about getting to church that each family member forgot

---

* Want to read more from Wooton? Visit *www.clubhousemagazine.com*, then hover over the Jones and Parker picture and the words "Go to Odyssey!" will appear. Click on the picture and then click on "Wooton's Random Ramblings."

Wandering with Wooton*

I have to be honest. This is the list of things I was
thinking about last Sunday when I was in church:
(1) licorice, (2) sea monkeys, (3) what items I could
put into a tuba to make it sound funny, and (4) God.
The problem was that I rushed out the door to get to
church. It works out better when I get up early and pray
before church. I'll try that next week.

the reason that they went to church in the first place. It took Tom Riley's good example
to show them that getting their hearts ready for worship was the most important task.
The Washingtons needed to do that before stepping through the doors of the church.

Whether you're praying, going to church, or singing praises to God in the car or in
your room, you should always give Him the full attention He deserves.

And He deserves it way more than P-Nut!

Daily Challenge

Write a fan letter to God. Make a list of the many amazing things He's done for you or
given to you.

• • •

Worship Theme Memory Verse—Psalm 99:5

Honor the Lord our God. Worship at his feet. He is holy.

Devo 66

The Names of God

Today's Verse—Luke 1:49

The Mighty One has done great things
for me. His name is holy.

D o you ever greet your friends like this?

"Hello, Boy-who-is-smart-and-plays-the-trombone."

"Good morning, Girl-who-likes-ham. How are you?"

"Doing well, Boy-who-wears-mismatching-socks."

Maybe not, but did you know that God has dozens of names that describe His character in the same way? In the Bible, God is referred to as *Abba*, which means "Father." Here are some other names He goes by:

- *El Shaddai*, which means "almighty"
- *Jehovah Jireh*, which means "the Lord who provides"
- *Jehovah Rapha*, which means "the Lord who heals"
- *The Alpha and Omega*, which means "the beginning and the end"

He is also called the Good Shepherd, the Light of the World, the Prince of Peace, Counselor, the Horn of Salvation, King of Kings, Living Water, Holy One, Righteous One, Savior, Teacher, the Vine, and the list goes on.

One great thing about all these names for God is that they are perfect tools for worship. One of the goals of worship is to remind yourself just how awesome God is and in what ways He is awesome. When you pray, you can begin with a name for God that has a special meaning for you.

For example, if you were sick a week ago, but then you got well, you can address God as Jehovah Rapha, because He is "the Lord who heals." If you have a fight with

Connie's Corner

I've been called a lot of things: *snoop*, *stubborn*. Eugene once called me *capricious*. (I didn't even bother to look that one up.) But I've also been called a few nice things, too. *Precious* (by my mom) and *lovely* (by Mr. Whittaker). I don't know if I deserve any of the bad names or the good names, but God has definitely earned every one of His names. So I guess I should use them, huh?

your brother or sister, but then later you're able to make up, you can thank God for giving you the ability to reconcile, because He is the Prince of Peace.

In the *Odyssey* episode "Hallowed Be Thy Name" (album 17), Whit taught about the many names of God. But there wasn't enough time for him to talk about every single name. And there aren't enough words in our language to talk about how wonderful our God truly is!

Daily Challenge

With your parents' permission and/or help, go onto the Internet or look in the index of a study Bible and find all the different names for God. What do the following names mean? El Elyon, Jehovah Shalom, Emmanuel, Rabboni, Rose of Sharon. Then think about all the ways God has blessed you. In your prayers, use a name for God that means something special to you.

• • •

Worship Theme Memory Verse—Psalm 99:5

Honor the Lord our God. Worship at his feet. He is holy.

Devo 67

Worthy of Worship, Part I: God's Power

Today's Verse—Psalm 18:2

The Lord is my rock and my fort. He is the One
who saves me. My God is my rock. I go to him
for safety. He is like a shield to me. He's the power
that saves me. He's my place of safety.

The competitors stepped into the ring. In this corner, the prophet Elijah. In the other corner, 450 priests of Baal. One versus 450. It wasn't going to be much of a fight, was it?

Actually, no. It wasn't.

In 1 Kings 18, God punished Israel and its evil king, Ahab, with a famine. Because Israel worshipped a false god named Baal, God kept it from raining in Israel for three years.

Then God gave His servant Elijah an assignment. God told Elijah to challenge the priests of Baal to a contest. Elijah took 450 Baal priests with him to the top of a mountain and said, "Get two bulls for us. Let Baal's prophets choose one for themselves. Let them cut it into pieces. Then let them put it on the wood. But don't let them set fire to it. I'll prepare the other bull. I'll put it on the wood. But I won't set fire to it. Then you pray to your god. And I'll pray to the Lord. The god who answers by sending fire down is the one and only God."

The priests prayed to Baal all day. "Baal! Answer us!" they shouted. They danced around for hours. They shouted louder. But Baal never answered.

Then Elijah prepared the wood and bull for his own sacrifice. And he said, "Fill

Loquacious Learning with Eugene

God's power allows Him to create awesome things. Did you know that the farthest star you can see without a telescope is fourteen trillion miles away? So if you were to travel in some sort of space vehicle going one hundred miles an hour, it would take you approximately sixteen million years to get there! That's quite a lengthy vacation. Stars visible only through a telescope are even farther away! The universe that God made is certainly a massive place. But God Himself is even bigger.

four large jars with water. Pour it on the offering and the wood." Elijah had men pour water on the wood three times. How could wood this wet ever catch fire?

Then Elijah stepped forward and prayed. Then suddenly God sent down fire from heaven. It burned up the sacrifice, the wood, the stones, and the soil. It even evaporated the water in the ditch!

The priests of Baal immediately proclaimed that Elijah's God was the true God. The priests had seen God's power at work and knew the truth. Then it started raining!

• • •

We should worship God because of His awesome power!

Daily Challenge

Make a list of the top ten things you worry about: It could be homework, disagreements with your parents, or arguments with your siblings. How small are those problems, really? Pray about each concern on your list, and ask your powerful God to help you not worry about any of them.

• • •

Worship Theme Memory Verse—Psalm 99:5

Honor the Lord our God. Worship at his feet. He is holy.

Devo 68

Worthy of Worship, Part II: God's Wisdom

Today's Verse—Job 12:13

Wisdom and power belong to God. Advice
and understanding also belong to him.

On April 29, 1962, US president John F. Kennedy welcomed a group of Nobel
Prize winners to a dinner at the White House. The guests were scientists,
mathematicians, scholars, philosophers—people with massive amounts of knowledge
about the world. President Kennedy looked at those at the table and said, "I think this
is the most extraordinary collection of talent, of human knowledge, that has ever been
gathered together at the White House—with the possible exception of when Thomas
Jefferson dined alone."

President Thomas Jefferson is considered to be one of the wisest men who ever
lived. His ideas contributed to the creation of the US Constitution, and as a result,
those ideas also formed the basis for what America is today. And yet Jefferson's wisdom wasn't perfect. Jefferson also owned slaves, so he certainly didn't get everything
right!

Do you have someone in your life who you think has great wisdom? Do you go
to certain people for advice about a problem? A parent? A teacher? A friend? A pastor?
Those are all good people to go to for advice, but their wisdom is limited. A teacher can
still be wrong. And a friend can give you bad information.

However, there is one source you can go to for perfect advice every time—God.
God's Word is perfect. If you go to the Bible with a problem, the Word of God will
never steer you in the wrong direction. What advice does God give? Advice like "Love

Wandering with Wooton

I was walking through the woods once with a friend, when he accidentally stepped on a beehive. The bees swarmed around him, and he yelled, "What should I do?" I shouted, "Roll over and play dead!" Oops! I got bees confused with bears. Sometimes I give bad advice, and so you should probably steer clear of me. I don't know if the Bible says anything about proper bee etiquette, but for pretty much everything else, it's the best place to go. I'm not.

your neighbor as yourself," "Don't worry about tomorrow," "Store your treasures in heaven," "Watch out for false teachers," "Serve others before yourself," and lots more.

There are tons of places to go for advice. Magazines and books hand out versions of wisdom. But that advice is often flawed. Go to God with your problems, and He will show you the perfect way.

You should worship God because of His wisdom.

Daily Challenge

Read through the book of Proverbs and mark down five pieces of advice God gives through His Word.

• • •

Worship Theme Memory Verse—Psalm 99:5

Honor the Lord our God. Worship at his feet. He is holy.

Devo 69

Whacked-Out Worship

Today's Verse—1 Corinthians 10:14

My dear friends, run away from statues
of gods. Don't worship them.

Sing it with heart:

My hair dryer is an awesome hair dryer.
It dries from heaven above.
With heat and power and love.
My hair dryer is an awesome hair dryer!

Is it crazy to sing worship songs to a hair dryer? In Bible times people carved figures out of wood and bowed down in front of them. They worshipped wood!

But as crazy as worshipping wood sounds, it's not that much crazier than what we do sometimes. We worship all kinds of things. Worship is showing honor to the things that matter most to us. And sometimes what matters most to us are silly things: money, our toys, television, video games . . . Are these the things we spend the most time with? That may be a sign we're worshipping them.

The *Odyssey* episodes "The Case of the Secret Room, Parts I and II" (album 2) showed how the love of money can cause harm. A man double-crossed another man over money and ended up killing him. Love of money ruined people's lives in that story, and wanting something more than we want God can ruin us, too.

As we learned in the Giving devotions, when it comes right down to it, all the stuff on this earth is going to someday be gone. Toys will break. Cars will rust. Money won't mean anything to us in the end. It makes sense to pay attention only to things that will

Connie's Corner

There was a time when I worshipped clothes. All I wanted to do was shop. The day I knew I had a problem was when I accidentally took a fashion magazine to church instead of my Bible! Now that I have to pay rent and bills, I don't have any money to shop, so I stopped worshipping clothes out of necessity. Maybe God is teaching me a lesson in what's truly important.

last forever—like God and His Word. Second Corinthians 4:18 says, "So we don't spend all our time looking at what we can see. Instead, we look at what we can't see. What can be seen lasts only a short time. But what can't be seen will last forever."

Worship the Creator, not the stuff or people of this world. Oh, man! My hair dryer broke!

Daily Challenge

While you go about your day, write down what you spend your time on. For example: "5:00–5:30, homework; 5:30–5:45, eat snack," and so on. At the end of the day, see what you spent your time on. And make sure you're not worshipping the wrong things by dedicating all of your time to something other than God.

• • •

Worship Theme Memory Verse—Psalm 99:5

Honor the Lord our God. Worship at his feet. He is holy.

Devo 70

Worthy of Worship, Part III: God's Love

Today's Verse—1 John 4:9

How did God show his love for us? He sent his one and only Son into the world. He sent him so we could receive life through him.

H udson watched as the basketball bounced off the rim. The buzzer sounded, and the game was over. He slumped down in front of his television. The one hundred dollars that he had bet on the game was the last money he had. In six short months, he had wasted all of his father's money on fun and gambling.

Now Hudson had nowhere to go. He had no real friends. All Hudson had was his father—the man he had betrayed months ago. Did his father even care about him anymore?

But Hudson had no choice but to find out. He sold his television to a neighbor and used the money to take a bus home. On the trip, he thought about what he could say. *Should I drop to my knees and beg him to take me in? Should I offer to work for him for free? Will he even look at me?*

Hudson walked down the long wooded driveway toward his home. He turned a corner around some trees, and he couldn't believe his eyes.

His father sat on the front porch as if he were waiting for Hudson. His father stood up, wiped his eyes as if he couldn't believe what he saw, and then ran—not walked— toward Hudson. He threw his arms around Hudson and, with tears in his eyes, said, "You're home! My son is home!"

• • •

Whit and Wisdom

Worship is an important part of the Christian life, and yet we often get confused about it. So let's go over a few basics. First, whom do we worship? We worship God and God alone. Nothing else is worthy of our worship except God. Second, why do we worship? We worship God because of His power, His wisdom, and His love for all of us. (And He told us to!) Third, how can we worship? We can worship God in many ways. In prayer, in song, by reading His Word, by giving, by listening, and by serving. Finally, where can we worship? In church, of course, but we can also worship God anywhere, at any time. At any point of the day, say a little prayer to God. Sing a song in your head.

This is a modern-day retelling of the parable of the prodigal son in Luke 15. In this story, Jesus gives us a picture of God's love for us. No matter what we've done, no matter how much we've turned our backs on God, He will never turn His back on us. He loves us and will always welcome us home.

We should worship God because of His amazing love.

Family Challenge #10—Church Service

Plan out a family-run church service. Have it on a Thursday night or sometime when all of you are together. Pick songs to sing. Play musical instruments. Read your favorite Bible verses aloud. Have someone give a short lesson or perhaps just read one of this week's devotionals aloud. Create a bulletin beforehand. Or you could listen to an *Adventures in Odyssey* episode about worshipping together. Make sure to pray together too. During the offering time, take up a collection and send the money to a charity.

• • •

Worship Theme Memory Verse—Psalm 99:5

Honor the Lord our God. Worship at his feet. He is holy.

Worship Scramble

Unscramble the letters to find the clue word. If you need help, use the Bible verse (NIV or NIRV) to help you. Then write down all the numbered letters in order below. You'll find another word for worship.

1. Psalm 23:1. A name for God.

    P E D R S H H E

    _ _ _ _ _ _ _ _
              4

2. Mark 12:41-44, especially verse 41. One way to worship God.

    G F I O N F E R S

    _ _ _ _ _ _ _ _ _
    3   9

3. 1 Samuel 18:6. An instrument used for worship in biblical times.

    O E A B U R T I N M

    _ _ _ _ _ _ _ _ _ _
    6

Puzzle #10

4. 2 Samuel 22:4. God is worthy of this.

I R P S E A

__ __ __ __ __ __
     1   7

5. Romans 11:26 (NIV). Another name for God.

V I L R D E E R E

__ __ __ __ __ __ __ __ __
2

6. Ephesians 6:18. A good way to prepare for worship.

R Y A R P E

__ __ __ __ __ __
     5

7. 1 Timothy 1:17. Another word for respect.

O O N R H

__ __ __ __ __
  8

Write down the numbered letters in order below. You'll find another word for worship.

__ __ __ __ __ __ __ __ __
1 2 3 4 5 6 7 8 9

Answers on page 242.

Going to Church

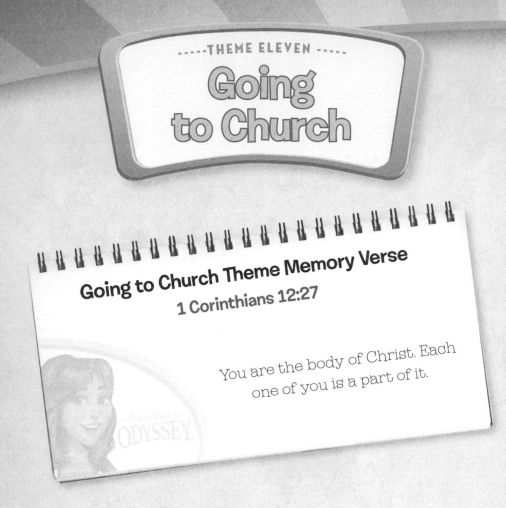

Going to Church Theme Memory Verse

1 Corinthians 12:27

You are the body of Christ. Each one of you is a part of it.

Ever wanted to call, text, Skype, Facebook, or chat with God? Well, you can't connect with God that way, but technology does give you options. You can read the Bible on your computer, you can be a part of a texting prayer chain, or you can chat with friends online about a sermon. Technology makes getting to know God and His followers a lot easier. Yay for Christian apps!

Technology can seem so good that you may even wonder why you need to go to church when you can watch a service on TV and worship God with songs on the radio. At first glance, attending a virtual church seems to make sense if you're looking at managing time.

But does it make sense spiritually?

What if your family went to an amusement park but left you at home to watch the fun from a live feed on your computer? Sitting in your bedroom, you wouldn't feel the same kind of fear on the roller coaster or have crazy hair after the spinning teacups. But you'd have seen and heard everything. It would *almost* be as if you were there.

Or would it?

Taking a virtual trip to the amusement park would be a poor substitute for the thrill of actually riding a roller coaster. In the same way, you can't experience the power of being with other believers by listening to a sermon on the Internet. Church isn't just an activity to cross off a list. It's not about singing praise songs just to say you've done it. There's so much more to gathering together with the body of Christ. This week we'll look into how going to church benefits you, and why God wants you to meet with other believers.

Prayer

Dear God,

I don't understand the part I play in Your body. Please teach me why it's important to meet with other believers in order to draw closer to You. I know You want what is best for me. Show me Your ways regarding my being a part of Your church.

Amen.

Devo 71

More Than a Building?

Today's Verse—Matthew 16:18

[Jesus told Peter,] "Here is what I tell you.
You are Peter. On this rock I will build my church.
The gates of hell will not be strong enough to destroy it."

There are many amazing churches around the world. Some kids in Iceland attend a church that's almost as tall as a football field. Some in Colombia go to a cathedral built in salt caves. The caves were created when the salt was removed by miners.

Our United States Capitol was used as a church from 1800 till after the Civil War. The persecuted church in ancient times may have carved stones into places of worship in the Cappadocia Valley of what is now Turkey. Then there's an Ethiopian church in the shape of a cross. It was carved out of stone underground, so its roof was even with the ground.

Jesus could have told His followers to go to special buildings, like the church in France that's built on top of a volcano like a plug. Or like the church in Rome that's made out of titanium dioxide and cement—a mixture that destroys air pollution.

But He didn't. In Matthew 16:18, He told one of His disciples, "You are Peter. On this rock I will build my church." Later, the apostle Paul wrote, "The church is Christ's body" (Ephesians 1:23), and Jesus "is the head of the body, which is the church" (Colossians 1:18).

The buildings we call churches are places for God's people to gather. God's church is a living, breathing, and active group of people who believe in Jesus.

In the *Odyssey* episode* "Tuesdays with Wooton" (album 44), Seth didn't under-

---

* Want to know which episodes feature Wooton? Or Connie? Or Whit? Visit *www.whitsend.org/vault* and find the area called "Browse by Character."

Loquacious Learning with Eugene

The venerable institution of the church is mentioned seventy-seven times in Scripture. The word *churches* is mentioned thirty-five times and is translated from the Greek word *ekklesia*. In three distinct places, the word *ekklesia* has been translated as *assembly* instead of church. It is clear that the word *church* is used to describe the people who make up a body of believers. It is not the building that houses them.

stand that he was a part of the church. Instead of showing God's love to Grady, Seth brought Grady to a building. Fortunately, Wooton understood and showed Grady God's love to Grady.

As a Christian, you are a part of the body of Christ, which is the church. So going to church is meeting together with other believers. And if you do it in a beautiful building, that's fine, too.

Daily Challenge

Draw a picture of your church. But instead of drawing a building, write the names of the people who make up your church and arrange them in the shape of a church building.

• • •

Going to Church Theme Memory Verse— 1 Corinthians 12:27

You are the body of Christ. Each one of you is a part of it.

A Part of the Whole

Today's Verse—Ephesians 4:16

[Christ] makes the whole body grow and build itself up in love. Under the control of Christ, each part of the body does its work. It supports the other parts. In that way, the body is joined and held together.

Perfect Pup Preschool is in a state of emergency. Somehow the puppies in day care all escaped and are running down the road, heading straight at oncoming traffic. You want to save the pups but suddenly find yourself in a dilemma. How should you complete the task? Should you use your belly button and belly dance them back to safety? Should you make a strange noise with your armpit to get their attention? Should you use your ear? Your ribs? Is this a job for your spleen? Of course not. You would use your voice to call the puppies back to safety.

You know what to do in each situation because you understand the different things your body is capable of doing. Some tasks are for one body part, and some are for another. The same is true about the body of Christ. Jesus is the Head, and His body is the church. The body of Christ serves others when every individual understands and uses their God-given gifts.

Some believers are the hands. They are good at feeding the poor. Some are the lips, and they are better at talking with people. The arms are popular because they give big hugs to everyone. For the church body to work, each part must serve and depend on the other parts.

Going to church helps you learn more about God, but it's also a place to practice serving others. If someone needs a smile and you're not there to give it, both that person and you lose out. John LaFete, in the *Odyssey* episode "The Boy Who Didn't Go

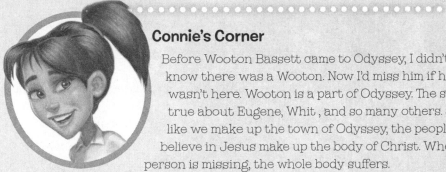

Connie's Corner

Before Wooton Bassett came to Odyssey, I didn't know there was a Wooton. Now I'd miss him if he wasn't here. Wooton is a part of Odyssey. The same is true about Eugene, Whit , and so many others. Just like we make up the town of Odyssey, the people who believe in Jesus make up the body of Christ. When one person is missing, the whole body suffers.

to Church" (album 4), had to learn this lesson the hard way. He wanted to do the jobs that belonged to other people, and he didn't understand how important his role was in the body.

Do you?

Daily Challenge

So many people have helped you become the person you are today. Thank your parents, teachers, or pastor for showing you how to serve others in the body of Christ.

• • •

Going to Church Theme Memory Verse— 1 Corinthians 12:27

You are the body of Christ. Each one of you is a part of it.

Devo 73

Listen and Learn

Today's Verse—Proverbs 1:5

Let wise people listen and add to what they have learned.
Let those who understand what is right get guidance.

In the *Odyssey* episode "And the Glory" (album 17), the Odyssey Coyotes went to the district playoffs. It was the first time their baseball team had done this in twenty-seven years. The whole town was excited.

Pete, their star pitcher, was unbeatable. In the first round, he led the team to a stunning victory against the Harrisville Hornets. But when Pete dove to catch the final ball of the game, he stretched the tendons in his wrist. To everyone's dismay, his pitching arm was placed in a cast.

Everyone in town wondered, *Who's going to pitch now?*

Pete was out. Dennis, the backup pitcher, had left for a family vacation. The only player who came close to being able to pitch was Henry, and Henry was scared. Fortunately, Pete knew what to do. First, he helped calm down his teammate. Then he answered Henry's questions and gave him pitching tips for the coming game. Pete even took the time to train Henry.

Henry followed Pete's directions, and to the surprise of everyone, the Coyotes won the next round. Everyone celebrated, especially Henry.

But then something happened. Henry stopped hanging around Pete. He stopped listening to the star pitcher. Henry started thinking he could pitch the next game, the championship game, on his own.

• • •

God has put people in our lives to help us grow—they are part of our church body. Sometimes we all stop listening to people who can help us, and sometimes we even

Wandering with Wooton

I'm not very good at baseball. Once when I was a kid in Little League, I was traded to another team for three bats and a snow cone. It was embarrassing. Christians are sort of on a team, too. Jesus is the Coach, and going to church is kind of like practice. And I know I'll never be traded. I love being on a winning team!

stop listening to God and His Word. When things are going well, we often tune out our need for others' help. And that's bad because we should always be seeking to learn from other people and from God.

If Henry had listened to Pete after winning a game, the Coyotes may have won the championship. But more than that, by listening, Henry would have shown Pete the respect he deserved. In the same way, when we attend church, we demonstrate how much we appreciate God and know that we need to listen to Him through His Word.

Daily Challenge

Listening to others is a great way to show respect and to learn how to live a better life.

• • •

Going to Church Theme Memory Verse— 1 Corinthians 12:27

You are the body of Christ. Each one of you is a part of it.

Devo 74

Rules and Consequences

Today's Verse—Proverbs 3:1-2

My son, do not forget my teaching. Keep my commands in your heart. They will help you live for many years. They will bring you success.

In a famous Swiss legend, the emperors of Austria sent a man named Gessler to rule over a Swiss region called Uri. Gessler liked being in charge of Uri. He liked showing his power.

Gessler forced the people in the city of Altdorf to bow to his hat. But his hat wasn't on his head. It was on a tall pole in the center of Altdorf.

People bowed because they didn't want to be punished, put in chains, thrown into prison, or killed. They obeyed this bad ruler to keep more bad things from happening.

When William Tell refused to bow down to the hat, he and his young son were arrested. Gessler said that he would set Tell free if he shot an apple off his son's head. William Tell did just that and eventually helped to overthrow Gessler and bring an end to his terrible evil.

Evil people make rules to control others and make them obey out of fear. But rules were never meant to be used that way. They were created as a guide to help us live good lives. We obey them not because we're afraid of being punished. We obey them because we trust the people who make them and believe they're for our good.

God is a King who makes rules to help us. One of His rules is found in Exodus 20:8–11. He commands His people to work for six days and to rest for one. God also wants us to learn about His laws so we'll respect His rules and won't accidentally break

Connie's Corner

One of God's rules is to rest. You wouldn't think that would be a hard one to follow, but sometimes it is. There was a time when people asked me to do stuff, and I couldn't say no to any of them. I grew so busy that I didn't do anything well. I've learned that I need to rest and meet with the body of Christ, the church.

them (Deuteronomy 31:12). Combining a day of rest with going to church helps us obey God and learn more about Him.

In the *Odyssey* episode "George Under Pressure" (album 22), George Barclay was doing too many things. His family had to remind him that rest was an important part of God's plan for his life.

Unlike Gessler, God shows us how much He loves us through His rules in the Bible. They have lasted for centuries. He wants us to rest and meet together with other Christians regularly. When we obey His rules, we're better able to handle the week's problems and joys.

Daily Challenge

Finish your schoolwork and/or chores before the day you go to church. That will help you rest and enjoy your church experience more. You'll be amazed how refreshed you are the next day.

• • •

Going to Church Theme Memory Verse— 1 Corinthians 12:27

You are the body of Christ. Each one of you is a part of it.

Devo
75

No Side Effects

Today's Verse—Hebrews 10:25

Let us not give up meeting together. Some are in the habit of doing this. Instead, let us cheer each other up with words of hope. Let us do it all the more as you see the day coming when Christ will return.

Scientific studies have revealed a hidden treasure. And you can share in it! What is it? It isn't gold or silver. It isn't a new drug or an expensive medical treatment. It's something researchers have found that will add three years to your life, help you get better grades, lower your blood pressure, and help you recover from bad experiences quicker. And best of all, there are no side effects!

Different research groups from all over the country have conducted studies on high blood pressure and depression. And surprisingly, they all came to the same conclusion: People who attend church at least once a week tend to have lower blood pressure, live up to three years longer, get better grades, and recover from depression quicker.

These findings surprised many researchers. But they didn't surprise God. He knows the importance of His people gathering together on a regular basis. When the body of Christ gathers together on a regular basis, good things come from it. The world now knows about some of the benefits that come from being a part of God's church. Perhaps someday they'll learn more about the spiritual benefits, too. When we attend church, we're drawn closer to God because we learn more about Him and set aside time to worship Him.

Wandering with Wooton

Is a sandwich really a sandwich if the bread or the middle is missing? If you take something away, it would just be "bread" or "peanut butter." Is a church really a church if the people are missing? People by themselves are called Tanaya, Isabel, Ben, or Jordan. But when they gather together, they're called the body of Christ, or the church. Which is way cooler. Excuse me. I'm hungry for a sandwich.

Daily Challenge

Do your own study. Ask everyone in your family how church helps them grow spiritually, emotionally, and socially. Then post the results on your refrigerator.

• • •

Going to Church Theme Memory Verse— 1 Corinthians 12:27

You are the body of Christ. Each one of you is a part of it.

Devo
76

Sticks and Strength

Today's Verse—Ecclesiastes 4:12

One person could be overpowered. But two people
can stand up for themselves. And a rope
made out of three cords isn't easily broken.

Once there was a family of five children that lived near a forest. The kids quarreled about everything. They bickered over breakfast. They picked fights at playtime. They squabbled over clothes, friends, and even toothpaste.

This brood of battling brothers and sisters fought so much and so often that their father finally yelled, "Bring me a bundle of branches!"

Before long, they brought him the requested sticks and squabbled only seven times as they did so. Their father took the large stack and handed it to his oldest son.

"Break this heap in half," he said. The oldest tried, but it was too thick to break.

The father took back the sticks and gave them to his second child.

"Split these sticks in half," he said to his daughter. She tried, but she couldn't.

The father gave the bundle to each of his children, but none could break it in half.

Then the wise father handed each child a single stick.

"Break it," he told them. Each broke their branch easily. He had them break more until the bundle of branches had been completely broken.

"If you stand side by side," said their father, "your adversaries won't be able to stop you. But if you bicker and battle and stand alone, you can easily be broken."

• • •

This story came from an old Aesop fable, but the moral is true today—especially for the body of Christ. Ecclesiastes 4:12 says, "One person could be overpowered. But two

194

Loquacious Learning with Eugene

The probability of being able to tear a phone book in half is virtually zero. But with the application of the laws of physics, you can rip one individual page at a time until the whole phone book is destroyed. This can be applied to the church. Our adversary, the Devil, will joust with believers, but he can't take on the whole church standing together, because Christ is the Head of it.

people can stand up for themselves. And a rope made out of three cords isn't easily broken."

One reason we go to church is because we're stronger when we're with other believers than we can ever be alone. With Jesus as the Head of the church and other believers standing with us, we aren't easily broken when problems come along. We're a part of something much bigger than ourselves.

Daily Challenge

Put five sticks together and try to break them. If you succeed, put six together and try again. Then put seven together, and so on, until you can't break the bundle. Look for the same number of Christians who will stand with you as mentors and friends when life gets hard.

• • •

Going to Church Theme Memory Verse— 1 Corinthians 12:27

You are the body of Christ. Each one of you is a part of it.

Devo 77

The Power of God's Presence

Today's Verse—Acts 2:42

The believers studied what the apostles taught. They shared life together. They broke bread and ate together. And they prayed.

Peter rolled over in his sleep. This was hard to do because he was chained between two soldiers. Other soldiers were standing guard at the prison doors.

Peter rolled again. Something had poked him in his side. He opened his eyes to see what it was.

A heavenly warrior stood in the prison cell.

"Quick! Stand up!" the angel said.

Peter stood, and immediately the chains fell off his wrists.

"Now, get dressed and put on your sandals," the angel said.

Peter didn't dare argue. He did exactly what the angel said.

"Now follow me," said the angel.

Peter followed the angel past two sets of guards. When they reached the door to the city, the door opened *by itself!*

Peter followed God's warrior down the street until the angel disappeared.

Suddenly Peter realized it wasn't a dream. He looked around him and recognized where he was.

"God sent His angel to save me!" he said.

Peter rushed to where his friends were staying. He found that the church had been praying for him the whole time he had been in prison. (See Acts 12:1–12.)

Whit and Wisdom

It's important for us to go to church and pray for one another. It's one of the ways we serve each other and add power and strength to the body of Christ. We also serve God by going to church. Not because He needs us, but because He knows what we need–and it's through the body of Christ that we can get closer to Him.

• • •

When the body of Christ—the church—gathers together to pray for each other, God's presence is there. Sometimes God will do things far beyond anything we can imagine. In Peter's case, God saved him from death.

Today we have the same opportunity to pray as a group for the people around us. Then we have the honor of waiting to see how God will answer our prayers.

Family Challenge #11—Make a Church

Build a church with your family, much like you'd build an inside fort. Use a couch, tables, chairs, and blankets. Then have your family stand together as a group. Which parts of the "body" did each family member play while you were building your church? Who in your family was most like the hands? Who was most like the head? What part of your family's "body" are you?

• • •

Going to Church Theme Memory Verse— 1 Corinthians 12:27

You are the body of Christ. Each one of you is a part of it.

Church Challenge

Read the questions and write the answers in the space provided. The answers are taken from this week's theme. Then place the letters with numbers beneath them into the secret message at the bottom of the next page.

1. Who showed God's love to Grady?

    ___ ___ ___ ___ ___ ___
       41 35   2

2. What did the five children do? (past tense)

    ___ ___ ___ ___ ___ ___
     20 36 23

3. What are the initials for Adventures in Odyssey?

    ___ ___ ___
    13 12 37

4. Who taught the five children not to argue?

    ___ ___ ___ ___ ___ ___
       16 33 24 40 38

5. Which baseball team made districts?

    ___ ___ ___ ___ ___ ___ ___
    10 25   1   9   15

6. What does the church have when it stands together?

    ___ ___ ___ ___ ___ ___ ___ ___
    27   4 21 11 14   3

198

Puzzle #11

7. What did the church do to help Peter?

$$\overline{32} \quad \overline{} \quad \overline{30} \ \overline{22} \ \overline{19} \ \overline{18}$$

8. What is another name for Christ's body?

$$\overline{} \quad \overline{29} \ \overline{5} \quad \overline{} \ \overline{26} \ \overline{8}$$

9. What does God want us to do with His rules?

$$\overline{28} \ \overline{6} \ \overline{17} \ \overline{31}$$

10. What surprised researchers?

$$\overline{34} \ \overline{42} \quad \overline{} \ \overline{} \ \overline{43} \ \overline{} \ \overline{} \ \overline{}$$

11. Which country has a "volcano church"?

$$\overline{39} \ \overline{7} \ \overline{44} \quad \overline{} \ \overline{} \ \overline{}$$

Secret Message

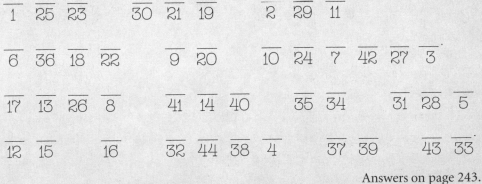

$$\overline{1} \ \overline{25} \ \overline{23} \quad \overline{30} \ \overline{21} \ \overline{19} \quad \overline{2} \ \overline{29} \ \overline{11}$$

$$\overline{6} \ \overline{36} \ \overline{18} \ \overline{22} \quad \overline{9} \ \overline{20} \quad \overline{10} \ \overline{24} \ \overline{7} \ \overline{42} \ \overline{27} \ \overline{3}.$$

$$\overline{17} \ \overline{13} \ \overline{26} \ \overline{8} \quad \overline{41} \ \overline{14} \ \overline{40} \quad \overline{35} \ \overline{34} \quad \overline{31} \ \overline{28} \ \overline{5}$$

$$\overline{12} \ \overline{15} \quad \overline{16} \quad \overline{32} \ \overline{44} \ \overline{38} \ \overline{4} \quad \overline{37} \ \overline{39} \quad \overline{43} \ \overline{33}.$$

Answers on page 243.

Serving Others

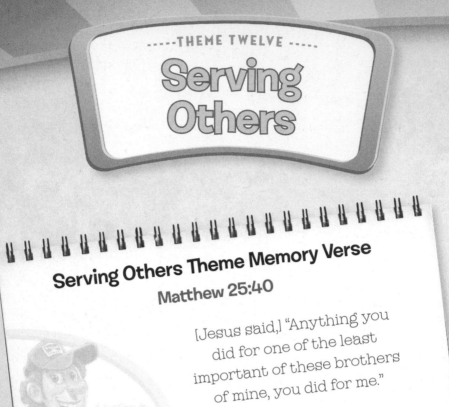

Serving Others Theme Memory Verse
Matthew 25:40

[Jesus said,] "Anything you did for one of the least important of these brothers of mine, you did for me."

What does it mean to serve someone? You might think of the waiter at a restaurant who takes your order, brings the food, refills your water glass, and asks, "Is there anything else I can get for you?" But there are lots of ways you can serve people. And whenever you do, you also serve the Lord. Jesus even said so!

One day Jesus was hanging out with His disciples, telling them about His future kingdom. As King, Jesus will honor those who have served Him well, His "sheep." When the sheep come before Him on judgment day, He'll say, "I was hungry. And you gave me something to eat. I was thirsty. And you gave me something to drink. I was a stranger. And you invited me in. I needed clothes. And you gave them to me. I was sick. And you took care of me. I was in prison. And you came to visit me. . . . Anything you did for one of the least important of these brothers of mine, you did for me." (See Matthew 25:31–46.)

Wow!

The message is clear: Whenever you do things for other people, you're serving Jesus, too. It may be hard. It will probably cost you something. You might not get a thank-you. But that shouldn't matter, because it's still putting a great big smile on God's face!

Prayer

Dear God,

This week, help me to think of people who need help. Guide me to people I can serve in big or small ways so that they will smile—and You will smile too.

Amen.

Love for the Least

Today's Verse—1 Corinthians 13:3

Suppose I give everything I have to poor people. And suppose I give my body to be burned. If I don't have love, I get nothing at all.

Our culture likes to rank people. World-class this. Top-ten that. You'd be surprised how many organizations have a Hall of Fame these days. Yet while people in our society make a fuss about the men and women it considers most valuable, they tend to ignore or brush aside those at the bottom of their list. Here are a few examples . . .

- Homeless people in dirty clothes, forced to beg for a meal
- Children in poverty-stricken countries who don't have clean drinking water
- Sick people with physical or mental challenges who need special care
- Lonely prisoners serving time behind bars after making bad choices

You can probably think of others. All of these people, written off as "the least important" by many in the world, are the very ones Jesus seemed most concerned about. In fact, He said that when we take time to serve them, it's just as if we're serving Him (Matthew 25:40).

Some Christians write a check to help out, which is great. Ministries and charities need money to pay the bills and do their jobs. Still others add a personal touch, working to meet the needs of others with their own hands. Have you ever served dinner at a homeless shelter? Donated clothes you've outgrown? Written to someone in jail? However you choose to love the least of these in Jesus' name, it can change people's lives forever and point them to the God who thinks they're world class.

In the *Odyssey* episode "The Amazing Loser" (album 54), Barrett gave his last two dollars to a little girl he believed would have to go without shoes. What happened next

Wandering with Wooton

Once on my route, I saw a man on the street who had a cardboard sign that said "Hungry." I complimented him on how honest he was, and then I made my own sign that said "Confused" and sat next to him. It turns out, he was hungry for a reason. He had no money for food. So I bought him lunch, and we ate together. He was a funny guy. It was nice to be able to help him.

was kinda funny, and yet things worked out well for the little girl *and* Barrett in the end. That's because Barrett showed love, and that's what God is looking for in an act of service. (See 1 Corinthians 13:3, which says, "Suppose I give everything I have to poor people. . . . If I don't have love, I get nothing at all.")

Daily Challenge

If your church serves meals to people in need, ask your family to participate. Or see if a local food pantry could use help collecting canned goods and other nonperishable items. Your school or a local business might even let you design a drop box and place it in the lobby.

• • •

Serving Others Theme Memory Verse—Matthew 25:40

[Jesus said,] "Anything you did for one of the least important of these brothers of mine, you did for me."

Devo 79

Me Third = Joy

Today's Verse—1 Corinthians 10:24

We should not look out for our own interests.
Instead, we should look out for the interests of others.

It was the day they'd been waiting for. George and Henry's big moment had finally arrived.

"After you," George said, stepping aside.

"No, no. You really should go first," Henry replied.

George smiled, "No, my friend, I insist that you go ahead of me."

This went on for quite some time until a gentleman stepped in and said, "Hey, you two, cut it out and keep the line moving. The executioner goes home in ten minutes."

Okay, maybe George and Henry weren't as unselfish as we thought. Still, humbly putting others first is usually a sign of a generous servant's heart. For example, suppose you want to play soccer, but you find out your friend has a sprained ankle. You may be tempted to say, "Oh, well, I'll call someone else." But how about offering to play a board game together instead?

Or suppose Mom has left you and your brother the last two slices of pizza. Do you grab the bigger one and launch into a victory dance, or do you let your brother choose? Serving others means considering their interests ahead of our own.

That can be a challenge, can't it?

A good motto for Christian living is "Me Third." Naturally, God comes first. Second, we should focus on the needs of other people, just as the Bible says in 1 Corinthians 10:24 and Philippians 2:3–4. Then it's okay to look out for ourselves. Another way to remember this principle is by using the letters in the word *joy*—Jesus, Others, You.

Since the Lord has promised to take care of our needs, that frees us up to look after

Loquacious Learning with Eugene

We are quick to demand our rights. We want the right to say what we want, go where we want, and do what we want. While it's profitable to have those rights and freedoms, it's nobler to lay them aside if doing so benefits someone else. The Declaration of Independence articulates that "all men are created equal," but the apostle Paul wrote, "Think of others as better than yourselves" (Philippians 2:3).

everyone else. So stand out. Be different. Decide today that you'll relax and trust God to care for you while you pursue *joy*.

Daily Challenge

Make a bookmark to use in your Bible or in another book you read daily. Design one side with the letters "J.O.Y." and the other with "Me Third" as reminders to serve others unselfishly. Be creative!

• • •

Serving Others Theme Memory Verse—Matthew 25:40

[Jesus said,] "Anything you did for one of the least important of these brothers of mine, you did for me."

Only the Lonely

Today's Verse—Isaiah 53:3

Men looked down on him. They didn't accept him.
He knew all about sorrow and suffering. He was like
someone people turn their faces away from. We looked
down on him. We didn't have any respect for him.

He usually sat in the corner. Alone. Quiet. Despite the many cliques in middle
school, no one had time for Mike. Oh, he was a nice guy—really creative and
smart. But nobody saw that side of him until he was gone. In the *Odyssey* episode "A
Lesson from Mike" (album 31), an accident took a young man's life, and Julie realized
too late why it's important to reach out to lonely people.

Do you know someone who doesn't have many friends? What's keeping you from
talking to that person at recess, or inviting him or her to sit with you at lunch? "But she
wants to be alone," you may argue. Are you sure? If she's been hurt, she may be protect-
ing herself. Deep inside, we all long to connect with others. It's just harder for some
people.

"But that kid is mean," you may say. "He has no friends because he drives everyone
away." That might be true. But when did Jesus say we should reach only out to those
who are easy to like?

Sometimes God wants us to serve others by gently invading their space. A good
first step is letting them know they're not invisible. Start with "hi." Then toss out a
question or two that will show you're interested in who they are—their likes, their
dislikes. It'll make them feel valuable. Once you discover a few things you have in common, you'll have more to talk about.

"But the kid I'm thinking of is an outcast," you may point out. "Being friends will

Connie's Corner

Do you sometimes feel lonely and ignored? You're not alone. I get calls all the time on Kids Radio, and my advice is simple: Step out of the shadows and let people see the great person they've been missing! God made you special, with gifts and talents to share. Serve others. Make your friendship irresistible. It may feel risky at first, but you can do it!

ruin my reputation." That's possible. Of course, the *right* people will respect you for reaching out to that kid—the Lord for one. Take a second to read today's Bible verse. Do you know whom the prophet was talking about in Isaiah 53:3? It wasn't the boy picked last for kickball. It's Jesus! Which proves that a misunderstood outcast could become your best Friend.

Daily Challenge

In the next few days, try to get to know someone who looks as if he or she could use a friend. Who knows, it could be the beginning of an awesome friendship.

• • •

Serving Others Theme Memory Verse—Matthew 25:40

[Jesus said,] "Anything you did for one of the least important of these brothers of mine, you did for me."

Devo 81

Set Your World on Fire

Today's Verse—Ephesians 6:7

Serve your masters with all your heart. Work as
if you were not serving people but the Lord.

Do you like firecrackers? Campfire s'mores? How about scented candles that make the house smell like lilac? If so, thank English chemist John Walker. Oh, he's not responsible for any of those things. But if he hadn't invented matches in 1827, lighting a fuse, a fire, or a candlewick would be awfully difficult today. Even though John Walker is no longer with us, he provided a service that lives on every time somebody strikes a match.

This week we're learning about serving others. Usually, that involves family members, like helping Mom clear off the dinner table or walking a golden tin of chocolate-chip cookies to Grandma's house. But God has also given you talents you can use to make the world a better place. Wouldn't it be great to cure a disease, design an amusement park, or write a hit song that inspires millions of people? Well, what's stopping you? After all, every world changer started out as a kid with a dream.

In the meantime, you can have a lasting impact on your school, church, or neighborhood. "How do I do that?" you might ask. "Should I pick up trash? Plant a tree? Become class president and campaign for jelly-bean Tuesdays and flip-flop Fridays?" Sure, you could go that route. The possibilities are endless. Do you remember when Eugene and Katrina created the nonprofit organization Hand Up? In the *Odyssey* episode "Blood, Sweat, and Fears" (album 47), they even helped the local hospital host a blood drive, and the whole gang at Whit's End pitched in.

No matter how you use your talents in public service, you should always put

Loquacious Learning with Eugene

When pondering one's civic duty, I am reminded of the words of Albert Einstein, who once said, "Only a life lived for others is a life worthwhile." Indeed, it is every Christian's moral obligation to enrich society. What do you think of this maxim for myself'? "Making the world a better place—one ukulele song at a time." Perhaps it needs some work . . .

people first, strive for excellence, and redirect any glory to God. Ask Him how He wants to use you. Then get ready to set your world on fire!

Daily Challenge

An everyday way you can serve your community is by yielding to authority. God has given parents, teachers, coaches, pastors, and government officials a lot of responsibility. (See 1 Peter 2:13–14.) By respectfully following their rules, you'll be honoring God. Is there a certain rule that bugs you? Ask your parents if the rule is biblical or not; if it's not, ask them what you should do about it. Also, pray that you'll understand why laws and rules are there, and ask God for strength to obey them.

• • •

Serving Others Theme Memory Verse—Matthew 25:40

[Jesus said,] "Anything you did for one of the least important of these brothers of mine, you did for me."

Devo 82

Ten Thirsty Camels

Today's Verse—Galatians 6:10

So when we can do good to everyone, let us do it.
Let us make a special point of doing good
to those who belong to the family of believers.

Camels drink a lot. Did you know that a thirsty camel can slurp up between twenty-six and forty gallons of water at a time? That's important to know if you're ever in line behind a camel at a drinking fountain. It also gives us a deeper appreciation of Rebekah's kind service to Abraham's servant in Genesis 24.

Abraham had sent his servant on a journey to find a wife for his son Isaac. Who would it be? They didn't know, but the servant set off with ten camels, most of them loaded down with gifts for the girl's father. After traveling awhile, he stopped near a well where young women drew water. He prayed and thought of a test. He would ask one of the women for a drink, and if she offered to water his camels, too, he would know that she was God's choice for Isaac. Sure enough, along came Rebekah, who gave the servant a drink and then said, "I'll get water for your camels too. I'll keep doing it until they finish drinking" (verse 19).

How long do you think it took Rebekah to serve this stranger? Let's do the math. If her jar held three gallons, and each camel needed about thirty-six gallons to quench its thirst, how many times would she need to fill her jar to satisfy ten camels? If you want to figure it out on your own, stop reading. If you're not a big fan of word problems, the answer is a whopping 120 times! Now that's generosity. That's sacrifice. That's gotta leave a girl's arms feeling like linguini! Rebekah had no idea there was anything in it for her. She was just being kind.

Wandering with Wooton

I can't believe Penny threw a surprise party to remember the day I converted from jellied cranberry sauce to the kind with whole berries. That girl knows how to celebrate an anniversary! It makes me want to rinse out her paint brushes and give her a jangly bracelet with charms representing PowerBoy's 121 symbols for "help." Doing kind things for people sure makes them feel important. And it makes life better, y'know.

If Rebekah could go that far to serve a total stranger, how far are you willing to go to show kindness to the people you meet?

Daily Challenge

Have you ever heard of an RAOK? That's a "random act of kindness," which means doing something nice for someone—maybe a total stranger—and expecting nothing in return. Make a list of fun ideas, and do one a day for as long as you can. How many days in a row can *you* go?

• • •

Serving Others Theme Memory Verse—Matthew 25:40

[Jesus said,] "Anything you did for one of the least important of these brothers of mine, you did for me."

Devo
83

Someone Else's Cleats

Today's Verse—Zechariah 7:9

This is what the LORD Almighty says: "Administer true justice; show mercy and compassion to one another." (NIV)

Sara Tucholsky had played softball for years, and yet she never hit a home run. That is until the day her Western Oregon University Wolves battled Central Washington. But as the ball cleared the fence and Sara began rounding the bases, she collapsed with a knee injury. It hurt so bad she couldn't move. She needed to touch all of the bases for her home run to count, and the rules said she'd be called out if her teammates helped her.

The Central Washington players could have seen this as a lucky break. But they didn't. Instead, first baseman Mallory Holtman asked the umpire if the rules prevented *her* team from helping Sara around the bases. Nope.

So that's what they did. "In the end, it is not about winning and losing so much," Holtman said. "It was about this girl. She hit [the ball] over the fence and was in pain, and she deserved a home run."

We need to have compassion for hurting people. That includes strangers, rivals, and even our enemies (see Luke 6:27). Mallory and her teammates understood that. As softball players themselves, they realized how it must have felt to be in Sara's shoes . . . um, cleats. Suppose your friend's favorite pet just died. Should you say . . .

1. "I'm really sorry. Are your parents thinking about getting another one?"
2. "Let's go shoot baskets to take your mind off it."

Connie's Corner

Once I thought I'd lost someone close to me. It really hurt. I just felt like sleeping until God made the world right again. Wooton was so sweet. He knew I needed a distraction, so he took me to the fair, where we played laser tag, ate funnel cake, and rode rides that nearly made us sick. My life has been a roller coaster ever since, but I'll never forget how Wooton tried to make me feel better.

3. "I know how you feel. I lost a dog once, and it still hurts."
4. Nothing. Just listen and maybe share a hug.

The truth is, any of those could be appropriate . . . or not. It all depends on what your friend needs to hear. And that takes sensitivity. God can help you serve hurting people in any number of ways. The challenge is knowing what they really need at any moment.

Daily Challenge

What Mallory Holtman and her teammates did for Sara was a touching act of sportsmanship. Search for "Sara Tucholsky" on YouTube and ask your parents to watch the video with you. Do you know someone who's hurting? How can you be compassionate?

• • •

Serving Others Theme Memory Verse—Matthew 25:40

[Jesus said,] "Anything you did for one of the least important of these brothers of mine, you did for me."

Devo
84

Follow the Leader

Today's Verse—Matthew 20:28

Be like the Son of Man. He did not come to be served. Instead, he came to serve others. He came to give his life as the price for setting many people free.

War is always hard. But imagine fighting in fourteen-degree temperatures and two feet of snow after your 128-man unit has been reduced to just nineteen healthy soldiers. That's the challenge American platoon leader Audie Murphy faced during World War II.

Did he say, "I'm in charge. You guys fight while I warm my toes"? No, sir! Murphy sent everyone to the rear of the line while he spent the next hour using a machine gun to hold back the German infantry. Eventually his men rallied and drove off the enemy. When asked why he did it, Murphy simply said, "They were killing my friends."

Audie Murphy was a leader willing to lay down his life for his friends. In John 15:13, Jesus described that as the ultimate act of service . . . and love. And He should know, because Jesus loved us by dying on the cross to save us from our sin. You see, leaders worth following don't think they're better than everyone else. Instead, they look for opportunities to serve, even if that means sacrificing their own comfort or safety (Matthew 20:20–28).

Jesus modeled this for His disciples by washing their dirty, stinky feet in John 13:1–15. They needed to see humble "servant leadership" in action. So our Lord grabbed a towel and a bowl of water, saying afterward, "I have given you an example. You should do as I have done for you" (verse 15).

Can you imagine the president of the United States washing your feet? How about

Whit and Wisdom

These devotions remind me why I'm so honored to serve people here at Whit's End. Not because I'm scooping ice cream, although that's fun. But really, it's because I have the chance to share what I've learned about God. I get to encourage someone, help people sort through their problems, or just be there to listen. That's what people need most. I can't prove it, but I'm pretty sure it even makes the ice cream taste better.

a Super Bowl MVP or a Hollywood superstar? Crazy, right? Yet the God of the universe has done that and much more by laying down His life to serve you.

Family Challenge #12—Foot Washing

Invite your family to join you for "a special event." Don't tell them you'll be washing their feet. *Yuck!* Don't worry; it's not as gross as it sounds. Put a little water in a large bowl. Soak a washcloth and place the bowl under their feet to catch the runoff. Then dry their feet with a towel. As you wash each family member's feet, tell that person something you appreciate about him or her. Be sincere. You are honoring them. Even if your brothers or sisters have trouble taking you seriously, make this an act of worship in the spirit of this week's memory verse. And no tickling!

• • •

Serving Others Theme Memory Verse—Matthew 25:40

[Jesus said,] "Anything you did for one of the least important of these brothers of mine, you did for me."

Servant Saying

John Wooden is considered one of the greatest college basketball coaches who ever lived. During his twenty-seven seasons at UCLA, this godly man inspired hundreds of players and even won ten national championships! Use the key below to decode a wise statement Coach Wooden once made about serving others.*

	1	2	3	4	5	6
A	H	F	C	B	S	R
B	O	L	A	U	I	E
C	W	Y	T	G	N	D

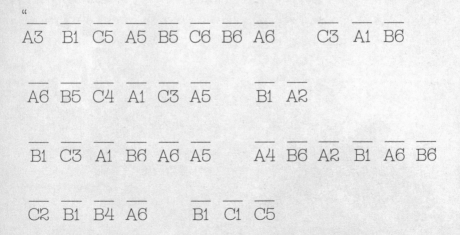

"
A3 B1 C5 A5 B5 C6 B6 A6   C3 A1 B6

A6 B5 C4 A1 C3 A5   B1 A2

B1 C3 A1 B6 A6 A5   A4 B6 A2 B1 A6 B6

C2 B1 B4 A6   B1 C1 C5

Puzzle #12

$\overline{A2}$ $\overline{B6}$ $\overline{B6}$ $\overline{B2}$ $\overline{B5}$ $\overline{C5}$ $\overline{C4}$ $\overline{A5}$, $\overline{B3}$ $\overline{C5}$ $\overline{C6}$

$\overline{C3}$ $\overline{A1}$ $\overline{B6}$ $\overline{A2}$ $\overline{B6}$ $\overline{B6}$ $\overline{B2}$ $\overline{B5}$ $\overline{C5}$ $\overline{C4}$ $\overline{A5}$

$\overline{B1}$ $\overline{A2}$ $\overline{B1}$ $\overline{C3}$ $\overline{A1}$ $\overline{B6}$ $\overline{A6}$ $\overline{A5}$

$\overline{A7}$ $\overline{B6}$ $\overline{A2}$ $\overline{B1}$ $\overline{A6}$ $\overline{B6}$ $\overline{C2}$ $\overline{B1}$ $\overline{B4}$ $\overline{A6}$

$\overline{B1}$ $\overline{C1}$ $\overline{C5}$ $\overline{A6}$ $\overline{B5}$ $\overline{C4}$ $\overline{A1}$ $\overline{C3}$ $\overline{A5}$."

Bonus: You may have noticed that each of the six columns in the code grid spells a three-letter word. Challenge each member of your family to craft a single sentence that uses all six words (and whatever other words you want to add). Once you're finished, share your sentences to see the different results.

Answers on page 243.

* If you liked these puzzles, you can find more online at *www. clubhousemagazine.com/adventures-in-odyssey*.

Overcoming Sin

Overcoming Sin Theme Memory Verse
Romans 3:23–24

Everyone has sinned. No one measures up to God's glory. The free gift of God's grace makes all of us right with him. Christ Jesus paid the price to set us free.

"So what's your class schedule like this year?" says Student #1.

"I'm really excited," replies Student #2. "I have first period Selfishness, and second period I have Disobedience."

"Oh, I heard that's a fun class," says Student #1. "The teacher sometimes has a hard time keeping control, though."

"I have Dishonesty third period."

"No, you don't!"

"You're right. I lied. I have that fifth period. Just practicing for the final exam."

We don't have to be taught to sin. It comes naturally to us. Every child who has had to take time-outs because he or she colored on the walls knows it. Let's face it. Sometimes sin is fun. But the consequences are not. And what it does to our relationship with God isn't fun either.

Sin is something we do that is against God's commands. Selfishness, pride, envy, disobedience, dishonesty, disrespect, and others are sins we all commit. And the results can change our lives in a bad way. This week we're going to learn about sin—what it is, how to avoid it as much as possible, and what we can do if we fall into it.

Sin can be a terrible habit for us, but it isn't the end of the world. God made sure of that when He sent His Son to die so that our sins won't count against us.

Prayer

Dear God,

Thank You for giving us a standard of behavior. Thank You for Your commands. Forgive me when I break those rules, and help me as I try to obey them.

Amen.

Devo
85

It's All Around Us

Today's Verse—Romans 6:12

Don't let sin rule your body, which is
going to die. Don't obey its evil longings.

MASH was a television comedy show made in the 1970s about the Korean War. In one episode, a Korean boy accidentally wandered into a minefield. Hundreds of deadly mines had been hidden just below the surface of the ground, ready to explode if anybody stepped on them.

A doctor named Trapper, who loved the boy, saw him and ran to get him. His friends yelled, "Stop!" Trapper stopped because he knew that the farther he ran into the minefield, the more dangerous it was. He stayed motionless while another man ran to get a map of the minefield so he could tell where all the mines were. Meanwhile, everyone shouted to the boy in Korean, "Stay right there! Don't move!"

When the man with the map returned, they discovered a very scary fact. Trapper was surrounded by mines. One step in any direction, and he would be dead. They called on a helicopter to come to the field, and Trapper and the boy climbed a rope ladder, got into the helicopter, and flew away. Until the rescue, though, they both had to stay perfectly still.

Do you ever get the feeling you're in a minefield, surrounded by sin? With stuff that's on TV, on the Internet, and on the covers of magazines at the store, and even with other kids talking on the school bus, it isn't hard to find sin. One step in any direction, and you could easily get caught up in it, or destroyed by it.

In the book of Genesis, God spoke to Cain. Cain was the son of Adam and Eve and the brother of Abel. God gave him this advice: "Do what is right. Then you will be accepted. If you don't do what is right, sin is waiting at your door to grab you. It longs to

Wandering with Wooton

So I have this friend. Let's call him Wooton for short. He sometimes has a problem with eating too much, especially when it comes to foods that have sugar as the main ingredient. This problem is called gluttony, and the Bible says it's a sin. Once when my friend was in high school and was nervous about a math test, he accidentally ate three boxes of snack cakes in ten minutes. That was four snack cakes per minute. Or maybe three. I don't know. Young Wooton failed the math test. Now when he feels like eating too much, he prays or sings a worship song. It's hard to think about food when you're also thinking about God.

have you. But you must rule over it" (4:7). But Cain didn't listen to God. He got jealous of Abel and ended up killing him. Sin got hold of Cain, and he was never the same again.

You have to make a choice. When you are faced with an opportunity to sin, you can step out on your own and play around with it—and you'll usually fail. Or you can stay perfectly still for a moment and pray, asking God for help, and He will rescue you. The important thing to remember is that you cannot fight off Satan by yourself. Satan is strong. You need to look to God to be your Protector.

Daily Challenge

Make a list of things you struggle with. Mark down the sins in your life that need to be addressed. Pray about them.

• • •

Overcoming Sin Theme Memory Verse—Romans 3:23-24

Everyone has sinned. No one measures up to God's glory. The free gift of God's grace makes all of us right with him. Christ Jesus paid the price to set us free.

Devo
86

The Consequences

Today's Verse—James 1:14-15

Your own evil longings tempt you. They lead you on and
drag you away. When they are allowed to grow, they give
birth to sin. When sin has grown up, it gives birth to death.

Hubert jammed his hands into his pockets and then forcefully pulled them up and
out of his pants. His face turned downward when he saw the hole in the bottom of
his pocket. His coins were gone!

He stood in aisle seven of the grocery store. It was the candy aisle. He had thought
about this candy bar all day at school. His mouth watered during science. He could
almost taste the nougat in his mouth during history. Now he had no way of getting
the bar.

Or did he? Hubert glanced around the store. No one was looking. He scanned the
ceiling for security cameras. There were none. *It's only a candy bar. That's seventy-nine
lousy cents*, he thought. His hand seemed to move by itself toward the brown wrapper.
Slowly it inched toward the candy bar . . .

So what's the big deal? Is anyone really going to miss a candy bar if Hubert steals
it? And even if he gets caught, no one is going to do much to a kid. So it's not that big
of a deal. Right?

Wrong. This is how sin works. The more we get used to sinning, the less we feel
guilty about it. And the less we feel guilty about it, the more we're going to sin. "Little"
sins turn into bigger sins. If Hubert takes the candy bar and gets away with enjoying
what he got for "free," then he might just decide that stealing is no big deal. So next time
he might steal a bag of chips. And after that, a watch. And maybe after that, a car. Hubert
could be heading for jail because he decided that stealing a candy bar was no big deal.

Connie's Corner

When I was ten, Cindy, one of my friends in California started getting into trouble at school. At first it was things like cheating on tests, and then it was stealing lunch money. She said that it was all fun and not really serious. But last I heard, she had gone to jail for stealing a car. Sometimes, you can't see where a path will lead when you start down it. But we know from the Bible that bad choices lead to a very bad end. I hope that Cindy learns that someday.

Does this happen every time? No. Hubert will always have a choice to do what's right. But Satan has a way of persuading us to do what's wrong. Letting sin become a habit is just one consequence of doing what's wrong. Romans 6:23 says, "When you sin, the pay you get is death." Sin causes death. Only through Jesus can we live.

But perhaps the worst consequence of doing wrong is that sin separates us from God. When Adam and Eve sinned in the Garden of Eden, their punishment was that they were separated from God. Sin gets in the way of our relationship with God. We can try to pray and read His Word, but sin has a tendency to always be in our minds.

Avoiding sin as much as we can is the way we stay close to God. The consequences are a lot worse than the rewards. It's just a candy bar.

Daily Challenge

Make it a point to resist falling into "little" sins today. Even if no one will be affected by it, resist the temptation to let sin get a hold of you.

• • •

Overcoming Sin Theme Memory Verse—Romans 3:23–24

Everyone has sinned. No one measures up to God's glory. The free gift of God's grace makes all of us right with him. Christ Jesus paid the price to set us free.

Devo
87

The Most
Important Person

Today's Verse—Galatians 5:13-14

Don't use your freedom as an excuse to live in sin. Instead,
serve one another in love. The whole law can be found in a
single command. "Love your neighbor as you love yourself."

Ananias and Sapphira were selfish with their money (Acts 5). Cain killed his own
brother out of jealousy and then claimed that he shouldn't have to "look after
my brother" (Genesis 4). Ahab killed a man because he wanted the man's vineyard
(1 Kings 21). David killed Uriah because he wanted Uriah's wife (2 Samuel 11). James
and John wanted to be Jesus' favorite disciples (Mark 10). Satan wanted to be God
(Isaiah 14).

The Bible is full of examples of people being selfish, greedy, and prideful. Philippians 2:3 says, "Don't do anything only to get ahead. Don't do it because you are proud.
Instead, be free of pride. Think of others as better than yourselves." In fact, almost
every sin that you could think of is a result of thinking of yourself more than others.

The consequences are pretty harsh too. Ananias and Sapphira were struck dead
after they lied about their selfishness. Cain had to walk the earth as a marked man the
rest of his life. Ahab's family was cursed for generations. David's rule as king floun-
dered after he murdered Uriah. Jesus scolded James and John for requesting to be considered the greatest disciples. Satan, who was at one time an angel, was kicked out of
heaven and forced to reign in hell.

Selfishness is so easy because the world tells us to be selfish. Commercials say, "Do
something for yourself." TV encourages us to do what feels good to us, even if it hurts

Loquacious Learning with Eugene

More than any other subject, Jesus talked about the sin of self-righteousness and greed. He often harshly scolded the Pharisees for sticking up their noses, to borrow the colloquialism, and believing they were better than others. His angriest moment was when moneychangers turned the temple into a house of greed. Personally, I believe Jesus taught on the subject so much because He knew that selfishness leads to so many other sins.

other people. Greed is normal. Envy is natural. Revenge is sweet. But none of these things are what God teaches.

There was a TV cartoon in the 1970s called *The Most Important Person*. The theme song went like this: "The most important person in the whole wide world is you, you, you!" What kind of a message is that? The most important person is you? That's not what God says. He wants us to think of others before ourselves. He wants us to sacrifice our own time, money, and energy to help others. He wants us to love our neighbors. He wants us to be unselfish. It's the key to joy, good friendships, and a better relationship with God.

Daily Challenge

Make an effort to be particularly unselfish today. Find someone to bless by giving them something, or helping them or sacrificing your time or energy to make them happy.

• • •

Overcoming Sin Theme Memory Verse—Romans 3:23–24

Everyone has sinned. No one measures up to God's glory. The free gift of God's grace makes all of us right with him. Christ Jesus paid the price to set us free.

Devo
88

"Getting Away" with Sin

Today's Verse—Proverbs 28:13

Anyone who hides his sins doesn't succeed. But anyone who admits his sins and gives them up finds mercy.

We never really get away with sin. For Christians, there are three truths about secret sin. First, it will haunt us.

In the *Odyssey* episode* "The Tangled Web" (album 1), Jeremy told his mom a lie about what happened to the money he was supposed to use for groceries. He actually lost it when he went to Whit's End without permission, but instead he told his mother someone stole it. The lie got bigger and bigger, and soon the mayor was giving Jeremy an award for bravery! Jeremy had a chance to confess his lie . . . but he didn't. Did Jeremy get away with it? Of course not. That sin will haunt him all the days of his life. Every time he looks at that award, he'll know it was based on his sin. A constant feeling of guilt is a terrible thing to live with.

The second truth about secret sin is there's a good chance it will be exposed. Numbers 32:23 says, "You can be sure that your sin will be discovered. It will be brought out into the open."

In 1989, evidence came to light that baseball player/manager Pete Rose had made bets on baseball games while he was managing the Cincinnati Reds. This is illegal and would have resulted in Rose being fired. But he denied it. For fifteen years he told reporter after reporter that he never bet on baseball games. Finally the

---

* This was one of the very first episodes, number 12. Want to listen to the Adventures in Odyssey episodes in order? Go to *www.whitsend.org/vault* and browse by album number, starting with 1.

Wandering with Wooton

When I was seven, I broke my mother's favorite necklace trying to teach my dog Barky to hula hoop (long story). I put the necklace back in the jewelry box and never told her. It haunted me for years, and I finally told her two years ago. I felt like a huge load had been lifted off my shoulders! Of course, she told me she knew the whole time. (I think Barky ratted me out!)

evidence was overwhelming, and he admitted to everything. Now Rose has to live with people knowing that he made illegal bets and lied about it.

The third truth about secret sin is that even if no one on earth ever finds out, the most important One of all will know—God. Proverbs 15:3 says, "The eyes of the Lord are everywhere. They watch those who are evil and those who are good." We should be more interested in pleasing God than anyone else. In eternity, we won't stand in front of our friends and families to be judged. We'll stand before God.

Even though God already knows our sins, we should confess them anyway—to God and to each other. It helps us realize what we've done, and it will help us do better next time.

Daily Challenge

Do you have any secret sins? Go to the people you sinned against and confess to them.

• • •

Overcoming Sin Theme Memory Verse—Romans 3:23-24

Everyone has sinned. No one measures up to God's glory. The free gift of God's grace makes all of us right with him. Christ Jesus paid the price to set us free.

Devo
89

Don't Fly Toward the Light!

Finally, my brothers and sisters, always think about what is true. Think about what is noble, right and pure. Think about what is lovely and worthy of respect. If anything is excellent or worthy of praise, think about those kinds of things.

Are bugs really that dumb? They see a light. They're attracted to it, and they begin to fly toward it. "Mmmm . . . light." As they get closer, they begin to smell something. *What could that be? Oh, I see. It's the electrocuted corpses of my friends.* Suddenly they hear a BZZZT! And one of their friends that just reached the light suddenly falls from the sky and dies instantly. If you were a bug, what conclusion would you come to? I don't know . . . maybe . . . *stay away from the light!*

And still, bugs can't resist it. But are they really any dumber than we are?

How many times have we fallen into the same temptation over and over again? We're tempted by sin, and for some reason, we still drift toward it. First Corinthians 10:13 says, "You are tempted in the same way all other human beings are. God is faithful. He will not let you be tempted any more than you can take."

Here are some tips for avoiding (or resisting) the "light." First, don't ever think you're strong enough to handle temptation by yourself. Don't walk into a situation where you know you may sin, thinking that you're fine. God will help you, but on your own, you're weak. Second, don't let temptation stick around too long. Cut it off as soon as you can. In the *Odyssey* episode "B-TV: Temptation" (album 49), there was a story about Mary, whose father told her to stay away from the heckleberry bush because it was poisonous.

Connie's Corner

I used to be tempted by gossip magazines. Every time I got in line at the grocery store, I would see the covers of those magazines, and most of the time, I would buy one. You know what I did? I started going to checkout aisle number four. It didn't have those magazines. That was my register, even if it had the longest line. I figured I would cut the temptation off at the source.

She didn't listen to her father, and instead of cutting it down when it was small, she let it grow. Soon it got out of control, and she couldn't get rid of the plant. Eventually they just had to build a fence around it. Don't let temptation sit there. Take care of it now.

Third, pray. It's harder to give in to temptation when you're in the presence of God. Pray or sing a praise song. Fourth, get someone to help you. Tell a friend about your struggles and invite him or her to ask you about it when you're tempted. It makes it harder to sin if you know someone's going to ask you about it later. Fifth, repent quickly. We'll talk about that in the next devotional.

It isn't a sin to be tempted. It's a sin only if you give in to it. God will be right there to help if you just ask Him to.

Daily Challenge

Make a list of your worst temptations. Decide on a strategy for removing these things from your life.

• • •

Overcoming Sin Theme Memory Verse—Romans 3:23-24

Everyone has sinned. No one measures up to God's glory. The free gift of God's grace makes all of us right with him. Christ Jesus paid the price to set us free.

Devo 90

Really Sorry

Today's Verse—Luke 5:32

[Jesus said,] "I have not come to get those who think they are right with God to follow me. I have come to get sinners to turn away from their sins."

Dear Joey,

I'm really sorry about what I did to you. I feel awful. Really awful. I wish I could make it up to you. I'm soooo sorry. Really. To sum up, I'm really, really, really, really, really, really, really sorry. Please forgive me.

From your really, really, really, really sorry friend,

Pete

• • •

Have you ever written a really, really, really, really sorry letter? King David did—Psalm 51. And he was *really* sorry.

David had just committed a terrible sin. In this psalm, David took all the proper steps to show that he was repentant. This means he was sorry for his sin and planned to turn away from it.

The first step in repentance is confessing your sin to God and others. In verses 3–4, David cried out to God in prayer, saying, "I know the lawless acts I've committed. I can't forget my sin. You are the one I've really sinned against. I've done what is evil in your sight."

The second step is asking for forgiveness. In verse 8, David pleaded with God, "Let me hear you say, 'Your sins are forgiven.' That will bring me joy and gladness. Let the body you have broken be glad."

The third step is turning away from the sin. Commit to avoid this sin in the future.

THEME THIRTEEN
Overcoming Sin

Loquacious Learning with Eugene

The word *repentance* comes from the Greek word *metanoeo*, meaning "to change one's mind" or one's purpose—and the change is always for the better. It implies a change in thinking, and henceforth, a change in lifestyle. In geometrical terms, repenting would equal a 180-degree turn from sin. Not 90, not 120, but 180—to travel in the exact opposite direction as the sin. When sin is at your back, that is true repentance.

In verses 10–12, David prayed, "God, create a pure heart in me. Give me a new spirit that is faithful to you. Don't send me away from you. Don't take your Holy Spirit away from me. Give me back the joy that comes from being saved by you. Give me a spirit that obeys you. That will keep me going."

David's reign as king was never quite as glorious after what he did. Still, the Bible never mentions David making the same mistake again. We all make mistakes. But those who repent of their mistakes will have the strongest relationships with God.

Daily Challenge

Pray about a specific sin today. Confess your sin to the person you harmed, ask for forgiveness, and ask God to help you turn away from the sin completely.

• • •

Overcoming Sin Theme Memory Verse—Romans 3:23–24

Everyone has sinned. No one measures up to God's glory. The free gift of God's grace makes all of us right with him. Christ Jesus paid the price to set us free.

"We, the Jury, Find the Defendant . . . Guilty!"

Today's Verse—Romans 5:18

One man's sin [Adam] brought guilt to all people.
So also one right act made all people right with
God. And all who are right with God will live.

"Did you break the garage window?" Nate's father said.

"No, I didn't," Nate insisted. "It was broken when I came out here."

His father looked at Nate with pain in his eyes. He knew that Nate had done it, but instead of grounding him for a week, he decided to use another tactic. "Okay. If you say so, I believe you. Because I know you're not a liar."

Here's the thing. If Nate had told the truth, he might have been grounded for a few days, but the punishment would have been over quickly. But he lied . . . and now, many years later, he still remembers what his father said. That's the power of guilt.

Guilt can be a really awful feeling. Strangely enough, though, guilt can be good. It means that the Holy Spirit is trying to help us. The Holy Spirit could also be called your conscience—that voice inside your head telling you right from wrong. The Holy Spirit convicts you of sin. He causes you to feel guilt when you do something wrong. It keeps you from wanting to sin again.

On the other hand, Satan can turn guilt into shame. Satan wants you to believe, "I lied. I guess I'm a liar. I guess I'm not worthy to be God's child." Guilt is about what you've done. Shame is about who you are. The sins you commit don't mean that's who you are as a person. Even if you do sin, you are still God's precious child, whom He loves.

There's even better news, though. God forgives all your sin. Psalm 103:12 says,

Whit and Wisdom

When I was in high school, a friend tried to convince me that cheating on a test was all right because "You're going to be a writer. What do you need to know trigonometry for?" There are plenty of ways to justify our sin. We can talk ourselves into anything. And Satan is whispering in our ears: "It's okay. No one will know or care. It's none of their business anyway."

That's why it's easy to understand why the Bible says we're "slaves to sin." But God has given us a way out. We can be free from the chains of sin by giving ourselves over to the holiness of God. How? We have to admit that sin is sin and ask God to forgive us. Once we do that, we can ask for His help to fight our sins in the future. It may be a struggle, but He will always be faithful and help—again and again.

"[God] has removed our lawless acts from us as far as the east is from the west." If you repent of your sin and ask for forgiveness, you won't have to worry at all about past sins. God has forgotten them. You can forget them, too.

Family Challenge #13—Confession Time

Even if it's awkward, tell your family about your struggles. They'll probably share their struggles. Start off small, perhaps, by telling your family or friends about "little" sins, but be willing to open up your heart and discuss some hard stuff, too. You'll find it helpful, and if you need an opportunity to heal from past hurts, this is a great way to begin.

• • •

Overcoming Sin Theme Memory Verse—Romans 3:23-24

Everyone has sinned. No one measures up to God's glory. The free gift of God's grace makes all of us right with him. Christ Jesus paid the price to set us free.

Puzzle #13

Stop Sin Scramble

Unscramble the following:

1. A 180-degree turnaround in behavior.

   P T E R A C N E N E

   _ _ _ _ _ _ _ _ _ _

2. Satan wants us to give in to this.

   I N T P E O M T A T

   _ _ _ _ _ _ _ _ _ _

3. The Holy Spirit makes us feel this.

   L U G I T

   _ _ _ _ _

4. Most sins are about this.

   N S L I E F S S S H E

   __ __ __ __ __ __ __ __ __ __ __

5. There are _____ to sin.

   Q O U C S E N E S C N E

   __ __ __ __ __ __ __ __ __ __ __ __

6. Sin _____ us from God.

   P T S S E A R A E

   __ __ __ __ __ __ __ __ __

7. King _____ repented of his sin.

   I V D D A

   __ __ __ __ __

8. God gives us _____ of sins.

   V S E N F S O G I R E

   __ __ __ __ __ __ __ __ __ __ __

Answers on page 243.

A Final Word from Whit

Congratulations! You've studied ninety devotions on the fundamentals of the Christian faith—that's quite an accomplishment! Along the way, you've learned about the lives of some amazing spiritual heroes like William Wilberforce, Corrie ten Boom, Rich Mullens, and Lottie Moon. And you've captured God's word in your heart through some incredible Bible stories about Jesus, Elijah, Paul, Peter, Silas, and Philip.

Of course, just reading about God and what He's done throughout history isn't enough. We have to *know* God, and we do that by meditating on His Word, communicating with Him daily through prayer, and living our lives according to His example. We need to become doers of the Word and not just hearers. It's also good to talk about the Bible with other Christians, to share what you've learned with friends and family, and to hear about what God is doing in their lives.

So you can see why the daily challenges of this book are so important. If you skipped over them, you should go back through the devotions and choose one or two challenges to try this week. Okay?

But most important, just because you've come to the end of this book doesn't mean your job of Christian learning is over. Far from it! Every day is an adventure of learning and growing in Christ. Being His disciple is a lifelong process; it's full of joys and struggles, study and understanding.

If you don't have any Christian friends, pray that God will bring some into your life. And in the meantime, you can visit Odyssey and Whit's End where there are always fun and learning going on. Connie, Eugene, Wooton and I will be waiting for you!

Puzzle Answers

Puzzle #1
Salvation Crossword

Across: 1. black cherry   4. salvation   5. Nicodemus   8. licorice   10. baptism   12. sun

Down: 2. Holy Spirit   3. fruits   6. gift   7. death   9. heaven   11. Silas

Puzzle #2
Jesus' Character Word Search

```
M I R A C L E W O R K E R A B Z T R
W D E Y O I U I V J F W O R L G C E
H S A C M G R L R O F M S T N N O D
O L O V P H E E P S I Q H I R H M E
S L A A T L D I L I L V F O U P E E
H L O C S O T M M E R I M O T S S M
E I I V S C H S E T G O I R S T I E
S G C G I I G R C R C O R S H O N R
A O S O O N E A O E C A L I L R T T
C F T T N M G F L M M I I S O Y F O
R O S O A R G I V E E I F R V T O T
I R A L T M S H U E R G H U O E G H
F G S H E P H E R D S M E R L L I O
I M I R L I U M E E E A P L T L Z T
C S H C A L M I O R R S I N L E S S
I H A R E M B R R E D E N R E R U H
N S V I L A L I V E R M I R L O V M
G W O R K S E H U M E R C C R E M L
```

Puzzle #3
Discipleship Quiz

1. Olivia 2. Wade 3. Frank 4. Lacey 5. Ethan 6. Owen 7. Logan 8. Madeline

The initials O, W, F, L, E, O, L, M unscramble to make these two words: **FOLLOW ME**.

Puzzle #4
Prayer Word Search

```
P R A Y Q N O K H C D V T T R P P T
C F Y X K P F K F K G A H E S Z X R
N I E M L T I O L W C N P C P J I U
O C C R O O Y C G A Q E C M W W P S
I V V E R N N A C N T U Y N S V T
S N N Q D E G T X T M S E R K N T S
S H T U S O B T I P F I W O W P M V
E E N E P S G H R U O L Z E K A Y F
F Q F S R S E A T W Q C Z G R P A J
N O I T A C I N U M M O C X P S T T
O P Y S Y S E K E F V H N W T A I S
C R Q U E U U S H V R J J I Z J D P
U R C R R E X G S D I N N W I W T F
Q B D T N I H I O I Z G B S P G K U
O Y N U L W Q V K B O X R D M S T H
B Y L H P E T I T I O N W O K M D U
J T G S Y H B N O D T S R R F N M L
J U Z A M D Y G L T D X Y D I O R H
```

Puzzle #5
The Bible Code

Lord, your word lasts forever. It stands firm in the heavens.

A	B	C	D	E	F	G	H	I	J	K	L	M
13			18	20	11		26	8			7	5

N	O	P	Q	R	S	T	U	V	W	X	Y	Z
25	24			1	21	10	16	6	23		4	

L O R D, **Y O U R** **W O R D** **L A S T S**
7 24 1 18   4 24 16 1   23 24 1 18   7 13 21 10 21

F O R E V E R. **I T** **S T A N D S**
11 24 1 20 6 20 1   8 10   21 10 13 25 18 21

F I R M **I N** **T H E** **H E A V E N S.**
11 8 1 5   8 25   10 26 20   26 20 13 6 20 25 21

Puzzle #6
Faith Find

1. B—faith 2. C—Einstein 3. G—dead 4. J—astronauts 5. H—Spafford
6. E—concrete 7. A—garment 8. D—praying 9. I—leap 10. F—stars

Puzzle #7
Ephesians Fit-In

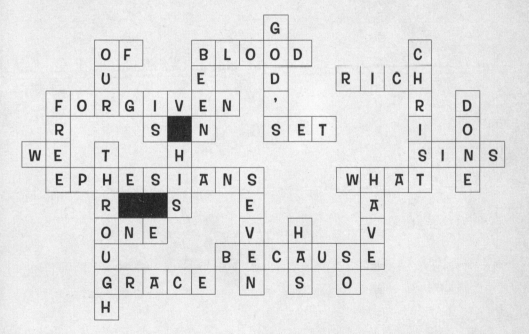

Puzzle #8
Giving Word Search

```
H C E T D O X J F U A T P Y T
B L E S S I N G S D G R T G S
C Y T I R A H C O I O I Y O U
D H G U M D J F K V S G F C R
L E E I E V O M I O H D Y E T
F N E E V P Y D R U A Y H Q O
H T R R R E E E G D R T S N U
N P Y S G F N O M Q I T I M E
Q V T R I E U P C T N X A B V
W M O V G S T L U I G B L K J
N P X P C O F D B A T B B V G
Z E D N T P A T Q I Z R P F B
P Z F X Q E X K R T G F Z X Q
T O X B N G X U K U D Y L G E
S U O N L X P I F A C S S U H
```

Puzzle #9
Witnessing Crossword

Across: 1. Paul   5. refrigerator   8. Moon   10. Holy Spirit   12. Philip

Down: 2. light   3. earn   4. fruits   6. opportunities   7. story   9. disciples   11. church

Puzzle #10
Worship Scramble

1. shepherd 2. offerings 3. tambourine 4. praise 5. deliverer 6. prayer 7. honor
SPECIAL WORD: adoration.

Puzzle #11
Church Challenge

1. Wooton 2. fought 3. AIO 4. father 5. Coyotes 6. strength 7. prayed 8. church
9. obey 10. findings 11. France
SECRET MESSAGE: "You are the body of Christ. Each one of you is a part of it."

Puzzle #12
Servant Saying

"Consider the rights of others before your own feelings, and the feelings of others before your own rights."

Puzzle #13
Stop Sin Scramble

1. repentance 2. temptation 3. guilt 4. selfishness 5. consequences 6. separates
7. David 8. forgiveness

FOCUS ON THE FAMILY®

Welcome to the Family

Whether you purchased this book, borrowed it, or received it as a gift, thanks for reading it! This is just one of many insightful, biblically based resources that Focus on the Family produces for people in all stages of life.

Focus is a global Christian ministry dedicated to helping families thrive as they celebrate and cultivate God's design for marriage and experience the adventure of parenthood. Our outreach exists to support individuals and families in the joys and challenges they face, and to equip and empower them to be the best they can be.

Through our many media outlets, we offer help and hope, promote moral values and share the life-changing message of Jesus Christ with people around the world.

Focus on the Family
MAGAZINES

These faith-building, character-developing publications address the interests, issues, concerns, and challenges faced by every member of your family from preschool through the senior years.

For More
INFORMATION

ONLINE:
Log on to
FocusOnTheFamily.com
In Canada, log on to
FocusOnTheFamily.ca

PHONE:
Call toll-free:
800-A-FAMILY
(232-6459)
In Canada, call toll-free:
800-661-9800

THRIVING FAMILY® Marriage & Parenting	**FOCUS ON THE FAMILY CLUBHOUSE JR.®** Ages 4 to 8	**FOCUS ON THE FAMILY CLUBHOUSE®** Ages 8 to 12	**FOCUS ON THE FAMILY CITIZEN®** U.S. news issues

Rev. 3/11

Start an adventure!
with Focus on the Family

Whether you're looking for new ways to teach young children about God's Word, entertain active imaginations with exciting adventures or help teenagers understand and defend their faith, we can help. For trusted resources to help your kids thrive, visit our online Family Store at:

FocusOnTheFamily.com/resources